HOW CAN I GET MORE OUT OF MY BIBLE STUDY?

Because the Bible is so rich we want to be able to absorb and comprehend as much as possible so that we can grow in our love for God, our obedience to Him, our understanding of ourselves and of the world in which we live.

Here is a comprehensive, understandable and practical book to help you understand and apply the message of the Bible for *TODAY*.

The Bible itself does not need to be defended; it only needs to be read and understood and applied by the reader. A genuine knowledge of the Bible and how to interpret it frees the Christian from any fears that some new finding will destroy his faith. The truth is not destructible.

A LAYMEN'S GUIDE TO INTERPRETING THE BIBLE

UNDERSTANDING SCRIPTURE

A. BERKELEY MICKELSEN
AND
ALVERA M. MICKELSEN

Regal Books

A Division of GL Publications
Ventura, CA U.S.A.

The foreign language publishing of all Regal books is under the direction of Gospel Literature International (GLINT). GLINT provides financial and technical help for the adaptation, translation and publishing of books for millions of people worldwide. For information regarding translation, contact: GLINT, P.O. Box 6688, Ventura, California 93006.

Scripture quotations in this publication are from the *Revised Standard Version of the Bible*, copyrighted 1946 and 1952 by the Division of Christian Education of the NCCC, U.S.A., and used by permission.
Other translations used are:
NIV—New International Version, Holy Bible. Copyright © 1978 by New York International Bible Society. Used by permission.
AT—The authors' own translation.
KJV—Authorized *King James Version*.

Published by Regal Books
A Division of GL Publications
Ventura, California 93006
Printed in U.S.A.

Library of Congress Cataloging in Publication Data

Mickelsen, A. Berkeley.
   Understanding scripture.

   Bibliography: p.
    1. Bible—Criticism, interpretation, etc.
I. Mickelsen, Alvera. II. Title.
BS511.2.M53   220.6'01   81-52231
ISBN 0-8307-0795-6   AACR2

Contents

Preface

In 1976 we wrote a volume entitled *Better Bible Study* (Regal Books) to help lay people understand the basic principles of interpreting the Bible.

Since that time, the need for this type of book has grown with the increasing emphasis on the role of lay people in the church.

This volume includes most of the material in *Better Bible Study*, plus a large amount of new material. Three chapters are entirely new: chapter 1, "What Can We Expect from Bible Study?"; chapter 5, "How the Bible Was Written and Compiled"; and chapter 13, "How Do We Build Doctrine and Theology?" All other material has been updated and revised.

This book also includes questions for discussion and exercises at the end of the chapters. These were suggested by users of *Better Bible Study* who wanted a way to test out immediately what they were learning. The discussion questions are not only valuable for independent study but are also of special help for those who use the book in Bible study groups, in

Sunday School classes, in midweek services, in adult seminars.

Much of the material in this book is based on *Interpreting the Bible* (William B. Eerdmans Publishing Co., 1963). That volume has been used primarily as a textbook in seminaries, colleges, and departments of religion in universities. This shorter volume is geared to persons who know little or no Greek or Hebrew and whose background in contemporary philosophy is limited.

A. Berkeley and Alvera Mickelsen
St. Paul, Minnesota

Introduction

This book has one purpose—to help the reader learn how to discover what the Bible means. Why do we need a book to tell us that? Why not just read the Bible and see for ourselves what it says and means? We can and should do that. But because of some special reasons, we may need some help.

Most of the books we read have been written during our generation for the people of our day. The writers share much of their readers' cultural background and thought patterns. When this is not true, we find the book hard to read.

Most people who use this book will not have a reading background in Oriental philosophy. Books in Oriental philosophy are available—written by Orientals. But even though such books have been translated into our language, they are often hard to read because the total framework of thought is strange to us.

When today's readers struggle through Greek mythology or Beowulf, or even Shakespeare, we must be constantly interpreting them. The words are the words of our language, but the setting is strange. The people think differently from us. They often have a different set of values. Even though we may recognize certain universal themes that are common to us in our day, we must make the transition from another culture and time to our own if the message is to be relevant.

The same is true of the Bible. It was written in a period roughly 2,000 to 3,000 years ago, in different languages and for people whose thought patterns, customs, and ways of life were very different from ours. The writers of the Bible were part of their generation just as we are part of our generation.

In studying the Bible, we are always confronted with these questions: What did this mean to the original readers? What does it mean to us today? In answering these questions, we are in the process of interpreting the Bible.

The Bible is by no means the only document that must be so studied to be understood. Volumes have been written interpreting Plato, Aristotle, and Kant. The archaeologist who analyzes the Dead Sea Scrolls must use every sound principle and skill at his command to determine what the writings mean.

It is especially important that we use great care in interpreting the Bible, for we are dealing with material of infinite worth—the very message and revelation of God. To the Christian, the Bible is the guidebook for all of life. It shows us the way to fellowship with God. It teaches what God expects of men and women. It is the one great record of God's full revelation of Himself in the person of Jesus Christ. Since fellowship with God is indispensable for a satisfying life, we dare not jeopardize it by a faulty reading or understanding of the Bible.

Incorrect interpretations of the Bible have had terrible results in days past. Erroneous interpretations have been used to support wretched causes, including racial and sexual discrimination, slavery, and particular views of science. One of the blackest chapters in Christendom appeared in the seventeenth century when the great mathematician Galileo was tried and convicted by his church for propounding the Copernican theory that the earth revolved around the sun as against the "scriptural" view that the earth was the center of the universe.

Why have such things happened? Because honest, conscientious people *confused the message of God with their interpretation* of the words of the Bible. The two are not synonymous, and it takes an honest person to admit that some of our deep convictions (often held with the most intense emotion) are based on a particular view of certain verses of the Bible rather than on the basic message of God given in the Bible as God's highest standard for us.

All Christians are constantly faced with the need to properly interpret the Bible. This volume will not give anyone a one-two-three formula guaranteed to bring "instant understanding" to difficult passages, but it will give some basic principles to guide our thinking and help us weigh the interpretations we hear and read.

How to Use This Book

Look up the Scripture references when the passage is not quoted in full. Only then can you practice what you are learning while you read this volume. Scripture passages are usually quoted from the *Revised Standard Version* or the *New International*

Version. In some instances, particularly in the chapter on poetry in the Bible, a more literal translation from the original languages may be given. It is often wise to compare several translations of the passage you are studying.

Think through the questions at the end of the chapters and work out the exercises given there. It gives you a chance to immediately apply and practice the principles discussed in that chapter. Only practice will give you skill and the satisfaction that comes with a deeper understanding of God's Word.

Study and read critically. You will experience a new exhilaration as you learn to make your own judgments based on firm principles, and the Bible will become more alive and powerful in your life. Remember, God intends for you to *understand* this remarkable book and to meet Him in its pages.

Chapter 1

What Can We Expect from Bible Study?

The Bible is not a book of magic. It does not give readers instant right answers to difficult questions nor foolproof green or red lights on hard decisions they must make. But most people who make a practice of daily Bible study find that it helps them to have fellowship with God, renews them spiritually for the demands of the day, and provides moral guidance for daily conduct. Can any other activity be more rewarding?

Unfortunately, some people approach the Bible expecting results that the Bible does not promise. Some expect every chapter to give inspiration and specific guidance for their own personal daily affairs.

A friend once complained that she was getting nothing personally helpful from her Bible reading and wondered what was wrong with her. We learned she was reading in 2 Chronicles. We assured her that what she should expect from 2 Chronicles was mostly a history lesson regarding the Hebrew people during a particular historical period. She would be able to see how some kings used their power for good and some for bad; how the Israelites went through long periods of idol worship and occasionally returned to God. It was not highly inspirational material. We suggested that while she was reading in sections like 2 Chronicles, perhaps she should also read one of the Psalms every day and a chapter in the Gospels where she would be confronted with the life and teachings of Christ.

She was relieved to discover that her failure to find deep inspiration in Chronicles was not an indication of spiritual coldness.

People read the Bible with other wrong expectations. Some read Revelation and Daniel hoping to find a blueprint of future history and to figure out if Russia or China is the anti-Christ or the beast of the future, and whether Christ will return this year or next! The Bible never pretends to answer such questions, regardless of how some "prophetic experts" try to make it do so.

Sometimes we want to escape from the responsibility of making personal decisions so we try to find the answers in the Bible. The Bible gives very clear guidance on some questions. The man or woman contemplating an extramarital affair need not read far to discover God's condemnation of such activity. But in other areas the Bible has little or nothing to say. What does the Bible say about scuba diving? Nothing, of course. How then can Christians know whether it is God's will for them to take up scuba diving? Such persons would have to look for broad biblical principles of action. The Bible teaches that believers are responsible to use their time and money wisely, to take care of their physical bodies, to put the welfare of their families ahead of their own.

One person might find that scuba diving takes too much time or costs too much for his limited budget. Others might find that the exhilaration that follows gives greater efficiency in their work for God and/or is a good activity to do with family members. Individual believers who honestly seek the mind of God in their lives must make such decisions after they "test everything; hold fast what is [morally] good" (1 Thess. 5:21).

Unfortunately, there are people who say, "Lord, guide me in this matter," then open the Bible and put their finger on a verse, expecting it to contain the answer to their question. On rare occasions, God in His mercy does give the needed guidance in spite of our foolishness, but that is not what we should expect from the Bible.

What Can We Expect?

What can we rightfully expect to gain from a conscientious study of the Bible?

1. God speaks to us about love, truth, justice, righteousness, and the effects of sin in our own lives and in the world. These teachings permeate the Old Testament—even books like 2 Chronicles. They leap from the pages of the prophets—Amos, Jeremiah, Isaiah—and from the Gospels and the Epistles of the New Testament. Many of the teachings of the Old and New Testaments are concerned with social justice— our responsibility to help the poor, the sick, the downtrodden of the world. Bible study confronts us with such messages.

2. God reveals Himself to us through His acts in the history recorded in the Bible. We see God's ability to deliver the righteous when He chooses; we see God using even unbelievers and pagans to accomplish His

ultimate purposes. God's greatest act of self-revelation, of course, is in the coming of Jesus Christ to this world, to live as a human being, to suffer and die for our sins, to rise again in victory. In the Bible we meet God in a unique way.

3. We can expect spiritual growth as we study the Bible and *apply* what we learn. Spiritual growth is not automatic in Bible study. Some agnostics and some very wicked people know more about the Bible than many Christians. Both study and application are essential for spiritual growth.

4. We can expect a growing understanding of God's standards of right and wrong. We learn how much higher God's standards are than our own. For example, our whole society seems to be based on a power structure. The desire for power permeates marriages, families, churches, governments, businesses. Our idea of success is to be at the top of the power structure—to have the final say on matters that affect ourselves and other people. The greater our power, the greater our sense of success.

Yet one of Jesus' teachings that is repeated in all four Gospels lays down exactly the opposite principle as the standard for Christians: "You know how the Gentiles [unbelievers] exercise authority and lordship over you; but it shall not be so among you. Whoever would be first among you must be the servant of all" (Matt. 20:25,26 *AT*).

In the Bible we find that God condemns adultery, murder, stealing, etc. But He just as thoroughly condemns hatred, lust, gossip, and backbiting.

For most of us, a study of the Bible makes us keenly aware of our own failures to live according to God's standards.

5. We are confronted with Christ. A study of the

New Testament shows us the person of Christ. We see His earthly life and teachings, and the interpretation of that life and teaching in the Epistles. Nowhere is the love of God so dramatically revealed as in the coming of Christ to give His life for us. A study of the Bible not only increases our sense of sin, but gives us the remedy for sin in the person of Christ. We can have joy and hope in our standing before God.

6. We can expect our Bible study to help us understand the problems of people in other times and how God did or did not respond to their problems. In a sense, the Bible is a "case study" book of God's dealings with people. We see God's mercy, His love, and His judgment in action. The case study method is recognized in all areas of education as being one of the most effective ways of learning. We have had it in the Bible for thousands of years, although we may not have recognized it as such. We *can* learn from the experiences of others.

7. We can expect the guidance of the Holy Spirit in our study. The Holy Spirit has promised to "guide you into all the truth" (John 16:13) and He will enlighten our minds and our understanding if we ask Him to do so. Seeking the guidance of the Holy Spirit in our study is not substitute for honest, hard work, however. The Holy Spirit was given, not so that we could be lazy, but so that we might know God and His desires for our lives.

8. We can expect fellowship with God in our study. Bible study often becomes a genuine worship experience in which we are overwhelmed with the wonder of God and our desire to praise Him. This is especially true in some parts of the Bible such as the Psalms, and in some of the hymns of praise in the writings of Paul.

9. We can learn more about ourselves and others. The Bible is an exceedingly honest, frank book in its details of the experiences of people. We find the prophet Jeremiah so discouraged that he says, "Cursed be the day on which I was born!. . . Cursed be the man who brought the news to my father, 'A son is born to you' " (Jer. 20:14,15).

Job, too, was so disheartened by the things that happened to him that he wished he had never been born. "Why didst thou bring me forth from the womb? Would that I had died before any eye had seen me" (Job 10:18).

In the Bible we see saints falling into sin, and we also see sinners such as Cyrus, king of Persia, doing courageous acts of justice or kindness (see 2 Chron. 36:23).

What Should We Beware Of?

If our realistic expectations about Bible study are to be fulfilled, however, we should be aware of approaches or attitudes that work against our gaining all that we otherwise could.

1. We can be bound up in the "scientific method." All of us are influenced by the philosophy of the world in which we live. Part of that philosophy involves the "scientific method" that assumes there is a cause-and-effect relationship in almost everything. In our twentieth century, everything that matters is supposed to be measurable in some way on some computer.

However, the principles of logic and research that may be applicable to the study of science, or even to the humanities, often are not applicable in the biblical sphere. But this is hard to accept because we are so accustomed to our cause-and-effect world.

Because of our mold of thinking, we tend to look for an explanation for every miracle and for every bit of predictive prophecy that was fulfilled. It is hard for us to deal with biblical materials within the framework of the times in which they were written.

2. We can be more committed to the religious beliefs taught us in our childhood than we are to the actual teachings of the Bible. All of us are conditioned strongly by the religious beliefs (or lack of them) with which we grew up. Ideas planted early are hard to root out—whether they are good or bad. In truth, none of us comes to the Bible with a truly open mind. Our preconceived ideas often condition the way we interpret the Bible.

Preconceived hang-ups are not new. Erroneous preconceived ideas kept the disciples from understanding Jesus' true ministry while He was on earth. The disciples, like the other Jews of their time, were convinced by their interpretation of the Old Testament that the Messiah had to be an earthly king who would free them from the rule of Rome. They could not conceive of a suffering Saviour even though Jesus kept trying to tell them what was going to happen. These wrong interpretations of the purpose of the Messiah have kept the Jews from the time of Jesus until the present time from recognizing the Messiahship of Jesus. The disciples themselves, after Jesus' death and resurrection, had to develop a new interpretation of the Old Testament. And it was hard.

That is probably what Jesus was talking about when He met the two on the road to Emmaus after the resurrection. He said to them, "Oh foolish ones and slow of heart to believe all that the prophets have spoken! Was it not necessary that the Christ suffer these things and enter into his glory?" And then,

Luke says, "Beginning with Moses and the prophets, Jesus interpreted to them in all the scriptures the things concerning himself" (Luke 24:25-27, *AT*).

For us, too, Scriptures that have been interpreted incorrectly or incompletely in our own childhood may make it hard for us to see what the Bible is actually saying on some important subjects. Our sense of loyalty to our early teaching can get in the way of our search for the meaning of God's Word.

For example, some people assume (because they have been told so) that later religious ideas are always more fully developed than earlier ones. If that is their assumption, they will find in the earlier writings ideas to prove that the God of the Hebrews is a tribal deity among the other tribal deities of other groups. They then look for evidence to show that ideas progressed from many gods to one supreme, universal God. Because they are looking for this, they tend to overlook anything that does not fit this pattern and to grab every shred of information that supports the idea.

Yet the biblical emphasis is on the tendency of people to wander away from God—not to grope toward Him!

We are all tempted to twist the Bible into the shape that pleases us and fits our preconceived ideas. Sometimes this can reach alarming proportions. For example, some have insisted that the Greek word *apostasia* (meaning apostasy), that is translated "falling away" in the *King James Version* and "rebellion" in the *Revised Standard Version*, actually means "rapture" in 2 Thessalonians 2:3: "For that day will not come, unless the rebellion [*apostasia*] comes first, and the man of lawlessness is revealed, the son of perdition." Making *apostasia* into *rapture* instead of *apostasy* is defended by a complicated appeal to etymology (root meaning of words). However, there is no support for any meaning other than "apostasy" or "rebellion" among the writers of koine Greek during the period in which the New Testament was written. The effort to find "rapture" in that word is made to support a particular theological viewpoint.

3. Our fear of paradox may influence our thinking. In the Western world in which we grew up, most of us are comfortable only with well-ordered systems of thought that give us tidy pegs on which to hang our ideas. Some statements in the Bible, however, seem to be paradoxical and since our minds find it hard to tolerate paradox, we prefer to ignore one idea and exalt another when the two cannot easily be reconciled.

This is especially true when we become enamored with some minor element of the Bible and then try to see that element everywhere. We can turn almost any passage into support for our favorite theme, losing our sense of balance. Under the illusion of being exhaustive in our study, we find support for our idea in places where a normal reading of the passage (remembering the original readers' situation) would give an entirely different meaning. Unfortunately, some such assumptions have been widely popularized. Most of us do not bother to look up the context of all the passages by which the writer or speaker supports his case. Thus we do not realize how many may have been taken out of context and misused.

4. We may practice "selective literalism"—the practice of selecting the commands we like and ignoring ones we do not like. Do we expound our belief that the Bible is "literally true" and then choose carefully which passages we say must be "taken literally

because it is the Word of God"? All the Bible is the Word of God in the sense that it is exactly the material God intended us to have in this important book that He gave to guide our spiritual destiny. However, few if any people actually believe and practice all the laws in the Old Testament or the New Testament. None of us carry doves to church to sacrifice on certain days of the year. We do not kill a red heifer or send a goat into the wilderness as a sin offering in keeping with Old Testament laws.

The same is true of the New Testament. First Timothy 2:9 says that women are not to adorn themselves with braided hair or gold or pearls. Yet almost every married woman wears a gold wedding ring. Braided hair is considered a very modest hairstyle today. In the same passage, men are told to pray "lifting holy hands" (1 Tim. 2:8). This is not our usual procedure. How to properly deal with such passages will be discussed in chapter 2 on "How Can We Know What the Bible Means?"

Unfortunately, many of us are so used to practicing selective literalism that we hardly know how to read the Bible without it. Selective literalism makes it hard for Christians to experience and practice genuine Christian unity. We all make different selections of what we want to practice "literally."

Since all of the Bible is God's Word to us, we need to study all of it carefully and humbly, looking for basic principles that should control our actions and that will give us a growing understanding of God and His people. That means we do not take "positions" until we have carefully examined all the evidence the Bible has to offer on a subject.

5. We may settle for easy answers to complex problems, even at the expense of the truth. All of us

wish that our many problems had easy answers. Few of them do. The Bible rarely gives easy answers to the profound questions of life. We often have to live with unanswered questions or with half answers as we continue to study and learn more about God and the world in which we live.

Many popular preachers and writers purport to have "God's answer from the Bible" for our complex problems, and Christians flock to these easy answers. Often, sometimes tragically, believers find that the easy answers do not work, and their disillusionment is severe. The Bible suggests honest answers, but not necessarily easy ones, to the complex problems of life.

How Should We Approach It?

If we are to gain what we can from Bible study we need to approach it with the right attitudes. We need an openness to new ideas. If we approach all ideas with a "fortress mentality"—that our main job is to defend the walls that make up the fortress of Christianity—we have very little space for growth. The Bible is a book of strength that has withstood all kinds of attacks during its 1,900-year history (nearly 2,300 years for the Old Testament). As in all other areas of study, scholars build upon and reevaluate the work of earlier scholars. We need not fear examining new ideas and evaluating them carefully in the light of *all* the teachings of the Bible, and under the promised guidance of the Holy Spirit.

We need an attitude of willingness to meditate on what we are learning and to think through for ourselves how our learning can and should be applied in our own lives. To do this, it is usually helpful to share our ideas and interpretations with other Christians for discussion and evaluation. We learn from each other.

Bible study is hard work. It is also exhilarating and life-changing. Study of the Bible can enrich us as no other study can.

Questions for Discussion

1. Do you think the doctrines you have been taught about the Bible regarding such things as water baptism, the baptism of the Holy Spirit, predestination, or the second coming of Christ influence the way you interpret certain passages of the Bible?

Do you think this is good or bad?

How can we have an open mind in studying the Bible and still have convictions about what we believe?

2. In what ways do you think our "scientific attitude" that looks primarily at cause and effect might influence how we read these parts of the Bible:

(a) The feeding of the five thousand (see Matt. 14:13-21)?

(b) John's picture of the Holy City in Revelation 21:1-4,10-27?

Chapter 2

How Can We Know What the Bible Means?

Most readers of this book are already convinced that study of the Bible is important. We can read it, and many have a regular program of Bible reading. But we still want to know what the Bible actually means by what it says.

One writer or speaker says the Bible teaches the necessity of war; another says it teaches pacifism. One person says the Bible teaches that women were created by God to be submissive to men; another says the Bible teaches that all are meant to have similar responsibilities and opportunities. How can the same book teach opposite viewpoints? Since there are differing viewpoints among Christians on many important issues of our day, how do we know whose interpretation of the Bible is right?

Because we all must stand before God to give account of ourselves, it is crucial that we have some basis for judging various interpretations of the Bible.

Sound Bible interpretation demands that we ask two questions of every Bible passage that we study.

Ask Two Questions

First, *what was the Bible saying through God's human servant to the first hearers or readers of that message?* The Bible was not written in heaven and carried down to earth by an angel of God. Rather, "men moved by the Holy Spirit spoke from God" (2 Pet. 1:21). Real people in specific times and places wrote or spoke to specific people about specific situations.

We need to try to put ourselves in the place of those first hearers or readers to understand what they thought was the meaning of the message. This, of course, demands close attention to the context (the general subject) of the passage. Some understanding of the history and culture of the time of the writing also helps us see what meaning the first readers would have seen. The message was written originally to those first readers and comes to us because we can learn something from the teachings or experience recorded in the first situation. The second question then follows naturally:

How should we understand and apply the passage (if it should be applied) to people today?

To decide, the Bible interpreter must understand that many of the teachings in the Bible fall into one of two categories: (1) highest ideals, norms or standards, or (2) regulations for people where they were.

"The highest ideals, norms or standards" are principles taught in the Bible that must take first place in our considerations and have top priority in all that we do.

"Regulations for people where they were" dealt with specific situations in a specific time and place and are not necessarily meant to apply to all peoples under all circumstances.

The Bible has hundreds of such regulations and they appear in both the Old and the New Testaments. For example, Leviticus 19:19 states, "You shall not sow your field with two kinds of seed; nor shall there come upon you a garment of cloth made of two kinds of stuff." Most gardeners in our day plant beans, radishes and lettuce in the same plot, and no one points to this verse as a law of God prohibiting that kind of gardening. And most of the clothes we wear are made of at least "two kinds of stuff"—perhaps a combination of cotton and wool, or linen and polyester, etc. Obviously, we do not believe this regulation has a timeless and universal application.

No doubt there was good reason for those regulations being given to the Hebrew people when they came out of Egypt to go to the Promised Land. What that reason was we do not know, but most Christians today are not even aware that such regulations are in the Bible.

Neither Christians nor Jews today keep the Old Testament sacrifices of bringing to God a bull calf for a sin offering, a ram for a burnt offering, cereal offerings mixed with oil, etc. Christians take seriously the message of the letter to the Hebrews that states that Christ Himself was offered "once for all" for our sins and that further sacrifices are unnecessary.

Even in the New Testament, there are some commands given to the church that most Christians now ignore, although the commands were very important to some people at the time they were given.

For example, Acts 15 tells that in the early church some Jewish Christians believed that they (and Gentile believers) must keep the Old Testament law as part of their Christian faith. Paul and Barnabas, who had been preaching the gospel to the Gentiles, believed it was not necessary for Gentile converts to keep the Old Testament law. The disciples discussed the matter a long time at a special meeting in Jerusalem, and then made a decision: "For it has seemed good to the Holy Spirit and to us to lay upon you no greater burden than these necessary things: that you abstain from what has been sacrificed to idols and from blood and from what is strangled and from unchastity" (15:28,29). This was the message sent to early churches made up primarily of Gentile converts.

Most churches in our time are also made up primarily of Gentile converts. Yet most of these rules are not a part of our church covenants or statements of faith. Why not? For reasons we may not be able to verbalize, we realize that these rules (with the exception of the one regarding unchastity) had peculiar application for the time and place they were given. They were regulations for people where they were.

Most of us in the United States are not faced with the problem of buying meat that has been offered to idols. But in the time of Acts, family feasts were often held in pagan temples using meat first offered to idols and then prepared for the feast. For a Christian to participate in such a meal could be easily misunderstood.

How about the regulations about abstaining from blood or from eating something that had been strangled? These, too, grew out of particular problems facing the early church. Leviticus 17:14 reads: "For the life of every creature is the blood of it; therefore I have said to the people of Israel, You shall not eat the blood of any creature, for the life of every creature is its blood; whoever eats it shall be cut off." In order to obey this law and to be sure that the blood drained thoroughly from any meat, the Jews had special ways of killing the animals and draining the blood. Strangling an animal was not permitted, probably because the blood did not flow freely.

These regulations of Leviticus were part of the daily life of the Jews of the time of the early church, and some of these Jews were among the converts to Christianity. The eating of blood or of anything strangled would be very offensive to them. Since common feasts and sharing food and fellowship were important in the early church, the Jerusalem council said that Gentile believers should refrain from these things that were so offensive to their Jewish Christian brothers and sisters. At the same time, the council declared that Gentile converts did not have to keep the rest of the Old Testament law.

Today in some countries food made primarily of blood is common. In Sweden, almost every store sells "blood pudding." It is eaten by Christians and non-Christians without anyone questioning it. No one in the United States asks how the chickens or turkeys we buy in the grocery store were slaughtered.

The only part of the command that most Christians still maintain as relevant to us today is the portion about unchastity (sexual immorality). That regulation is repeated in many other sections of the New Testament and by Christ Himself. He condemned not only extramarital sex, but also the lust that usually precedes it. This becomes part of our "highest norms or standards."

Which Is Which?

The basic question we must face is this: How can we distinguish between "highest norms or standards" and "regulations for people where they were"?

This is *not* simply a matter of "what I like versus what you like." There may be room for some differences of opinion—but not as many as we might think.

First, highest norms or standards were emphasized by both Jesus Christ and by the Apostle Paul and were sometimes plainly stated as being the highest standard. For example, when Jesus taught the Golden Rule He stated flatly that it was the highest absolute standard. "In everything, do to others what you would have them do to you, for *this sums up the Law and the Prophets*" (Matt. 7:12, *NIV*, italics added).

The same thing appears in the discussion about the Greatest Commandment. "One of them [a Sadducee], an expert in the law, tested him with this question: 'Teacher, which is the greatest commandment in the Law?'

"Jesus replied, ' "Love the Lord your God with all your heart and with all your soul and with all your mind." This is the first and greatest commandment. And the second is like it: "Love your neighbor as yourself." *All the Law and the Prophets hang on these two commandments*' " (Matt. 22:35-40, *NIV*, italics added).

Jesus was, of course, reiterating and strengthening the statement in Leviticus 19:18: "You shall love your neighbor as yourself: I am the Lord."

The Apostle Paul gives the same idea in Romans 13:8-10: "Let no debt remain outstanding, except the continuing debt to love one another, for he who loves his fellow man has fulfilled the law. The commandments, 'Do not commit adultery,' 'Do not murder,' 'Do not steal,' 'Do not covet,' and whatever other commandment there may be, are summed up in this one rule: 'Love your neighbor as yourself.' Love does no harm to its neighbor. Therefore love is the fulfillment of the law" (*NIV*).

Old Testament and New Testament regulations that seem contrary to these basic "highest standards" so clearly taught by Jesus and His apostle, Paul, must be carefully examined to see whether they fall into the category of "regulations for people where they were" because of some specific local or temporary situation. For example, any regulation of the Bible that seems to make one group of Christians of lesser rank than another group (whether because of race, sex, age, or economic status) must be examined to see whether it follows the highest standard of treating others the way we want to be treated or whether it was a temporary or local regulation for people where they were.

Another test of highest standards is found in connection with statements about the purpose of Christ's ministry and the purpose of the gospel.

Jesus said He came to bring abundant life to those who follow Him. "I have come that they may have life, and have it to the full" (John 10:10, *NIV*). Regulations that diminish opportunities for spiritual growth and service are automatically suspect, since they run counter to the highest standard of promoting the abundant life that Jesus said He came to bring.

Third, highest standards demand that Christians have a growing understanding of the *new order* that Jesus proclaimed—new wine must be placed in new wineskins. "No one sews a patch of unshrunk cloth on an old garment, for the patch will pull away from the garment, making the tear worse. Neither do men pour new wine into old wineskins. If they do, the skins will burst, the wine will run out and the wineskins will be ruined. No, they pour new wine into new wineskins, and both are preserved" (Matt. 9:16,17 *NIV*).

The gospel of new life in Christ is "new wine" that must not be poured into the old wineskins of Judaism or of paganism or secularism. The Holy Spirit came to give new power to the young church so that the abundant life in Christ could be fully realized.

But the new order that Christ came to bring often runs counter to the pattern of today's secular world and of ancient Judaism and may seem almost incomprehensible to us. For example, patterns of earthly authority in the time of Christ were very similar to patterns of earthly authority with which we are familiar. But Jesus gave an entirely different pattern which He said was to be normative for His followers— the pattern of servanthood. Christ not only taught what true leadership and authority are, but He demonstrated them in His own life by persistently taking the servant role among His disciples and finally giving His life "as a ransom for all."

Selective literalism in interpreting the Bible can be and has been used to make the Bible support causes that are far removed from the highest ideas and standards taught by Christ. These include such sad stories as the condemnation of Galileo for his discovery that the earth revolved around the sun because "the Bible taught" that the sun once stood still in the time of Joshua. About 150 years ago, many in the "Bible belt" of our country insisted that the Bible approved and ordained slavery because Paul told slaves to be obedient to their masters (Eph. 6:5) and that "each one should remain in the situation which he was in when God called him" (1 Cor. 7:20, *NIV*).

Sound Bible interpretation demands that we understand the difference between highest standards and the regulations for people where they were. We must try to see what the original message was for the first hearers and readers. We must consider the context of every passage and seek the guidance of the Holy Spirit to hear and understand what the Scriptures are saying to us.

Questions for Discussion

1. Do you think our emphasis on individualism in the United States makes us read Ephesians 1:15-21 differently from the way Christians at Ephesus may have read it?

2. Read 1 Timothy 5. Which portions of this chapter do you think represent regulations for people where they were and which state highest standards or illustrate highest standards found elsewhere in the Bible?

Chapter 3

What Makes the Bible Different?

Is the Bible different from other books? Yes and No. In some important ways it is like other books; in some important ways it is different.

The Bible, like other books, was written by people in specific historical situations, in specific geographical places, and in specific cultural milieus that influenced their thinking. The Bible was not written in a social and historical vacuum. For example, Paul's letter to Philemon addresses a crisis between a runaway slave and his master. This was a common occurrence in that historical time and place. What Paul said, however, illuminates significant truths about the gospel and has a message for us in our day.

The Bible, like other writings, reveals the varying literary styles of its human authors. Among the various writers there are significant differences in vocabulary, smoothness of style, difficulty of language. The Gospel of Luke and the book of Acts have more extensive Greek vocabulary than many other New Testament books. The second epistle of Peter is known among Greek scholars for its difficult sentence structure.

The Bible, like other ancient writings, involves many forms of literature such as history, poetry, parables, letters, and apocalyptic writings. The Bible includes extensive history about the Hebrew people, about the life of Christ and about the early church. It also includes some of the world's greatest poetry, such as the Psalms and the book of Job. Among famous letters, few have been read by so many people and studied so intently as the letters of Paul in the New Testament.

But the Bible is also different from other books in significant ways. The primary difference is that the Bible is a book with a message that uniquely meets the needs of people. This is its message: God desires fellowship with us and God has provided the means by which such fellowship is possible.

The Bible not only has this unique message, but it claims authority from God with that message. Its writers claim divine inspiration.

The Bible Claims Authority from God

The Bible derives its authority from God Himself. He is the God who acts; He is the God who speaks. Throughout the Old Testament, the writers insist that God speaks—sometimes to the prophet or to the king or to the priest or to the people. Sometimes God speaks to all four at the same time, as in the days of Huldah, the prophet. Josiah, the godly king, sent Hilkiah, the priest, to Huldah, the prophet, to hear the word of God to be transmitted to the people (2 Kings 22:1—23:25).

In the Old Testament, several basic Hebrew words or phrases are used to declare that God is speaking.

One is the expression *neum* which appears in several variations, all having to do with the utterance or declaration of God, such as: "The utterance of the Lord of hosts," "the utterance of God, Lord of hosts" and "the utterance of the King whose name is Lord of hosts." This term "utterance" referring to God appears 366 times in the Old Testament—usually in the prophets. It is used in Jeremiah more than 100 times, and in Ezekiel eighty-five times. Each time, the context stresses that the declaration is made by the Lord who has called people to hear what He is saying to them.

Another Hebrew word, *amar*, means "to speak." This word usually appears in phrases such as, "Thus says the Lord, the God of Israel"; "thus said the high and lofty one."

The common Hebrew word *davar* also means "speak." This is used often of ordinary speech, but also appears frequently when the speaker is the Lord. This verb appears 525 times in the Old Testament. Like *amar* and *neum*, *davar* is often used when God is speaking judgment or blessing on His people in a way showing that God was present among them.

Davar is also used as a noun meaning "speech" or "word." It is used 394 times in the Old Testament in reference to "the word of God."

The New Testament has the same ring of authority as the Old Testament. Jesus proclaimed good news and His hearers said, "No man ever spoke like this man!" (John 7:46). Jesus also performed miraculous deeds, and the events of His life were without parallel. "We never saw anything like this!" said one onlooker (Mark 2:12). Yet such events, unparalleled though they were, were overshadowed by Jesus' death and resurrection.

The authority of the New Testament lies in the

person of Jesus Christ—His acts, His words, and His disciples' proclamation of the good news of the gospel.

The Bible Claims Inspiration

Any discussion about the inspiration of the Bible must consider two important factors: First, what did the writers of the Scriptures say about its inspiration? Second, what do their writings show about the nature of inspiration?

The biblical writers say that God's action brought the Old Testament Scriptures into being. Paul wrote: "All scripture is inspired of God and is profitable for teaching, for reproof, for correction (involving restoration) and for training (disciplined instruction) in righteousness, that God's person may be proficient, having been equipped (furnished) for every good work" (2 Tim. 3:16,17, *AT*). Peter wrote, "First of all you must understand this, that no prophecy of scripture is a matter of one's own interpretation, because no prophecy ever came by the impulse of man, but men moved by the Holy Spirit spoke from God" (2 Pet. 1:20,21).

When Paul wrote his letter to Timothy, and when Peter wrote his epistle, they were referring to the Old Testament as "Scripture." Those were the Scriptures that they knew about. However, the same processes that had given agreement regarding which writings were to be included in the Old Testament later came into play regarding the New Testament, and Paul's and Peter's statements about the inspiration of the Scriptures became part of the New Testament. (See chap. 4, "How the Bible Was Written and Compiled.")

Both Paul and Peter seem to present inspiration as a God-directed sense of urgency and message, in which the human authors were energized and directed by the Holy Spirit. We might say the Bible was co-authored—with God in control.

"Verbal inspiration" refers to language inspiration, involving a meaningful association of words in the author's thought pattern. Perhaps Paul had this in mind when he wrote to the Corinthians, "And we impart this in words not taught by human wisdom but taught by the Spirit" (1 Cor. 2:13).

In many of the Old Testament prophets, and in Paul, there is the sense that the *message* was inspired—whether it was given orally or in written form. Peter wrote that "men moved by the Holy Spirit *spoke* from God." In our time when we are flooded with printed material, we can hardly realize the importance of *oral* messages in societies that had no printing presses. Most of the inspired messages of the Old Testament prophets were first delivered to the people by word of mouth and only later written down.

This sense of God's inspiration in oral messages is also confirmed by Paul when he wrote to the Thessalonians: "And we also thank God constantly for this, that when you received the word of God which you *heard* from us, you accepted it not as the word of men but as what it really is, the word of God, which is at work in you believers" (1 Thess. 2:13, italics added).

Paul apparently believed that his *spoken* word involving the gospel was just as inspired of God as his written words. Here Paul stands on the same ground as the Old Testament prophets.

The "how" of inspiration is not clearly stated in the Bible. The Bible clearly claims to be inspired of God. But how exactly did that inspiration work? Did the human authors sit down and write what the Spirit of God whispered in their ears, much as a secretary writes what the employer dictates? Apparently not, for the writers exhibit great differences in style and vocabulary.

Does inspiration mean that all material came directly from God in visions or divine whisperings, apart from any human source? Not at all. The whole Bible is God's word in men's language. Further, the Bible is co-authored, with God in control.

God did often reveal Himself and truth about Himself to His servants in dreams, visions, and other means. And sometimes God apparently supplied to His inspired servants the interpretations of significant events, such as the death and resurrection of Christ. The meaning of these events come to us from the letters in the New Testament as well as from the Gospels.

Writers of Scriptures, however, also often used materials from their own times and cultures. They used source materials available to them in documents and information handed down by word of mouth. For example, Luke prefaces his Gospel with the words, "Inasmuch as many have undertaken to compile a narrative of the things which have been accomplished among us, just as they were delivered to us by those who from the beginning were eyewitnesses and ministers of the word, it seemed good to me also, having followed all things closely for some time past, to write an orderly account for you, most excellent Theophilus, that you may know the truth concerning the things of which you have been informed" (Luke 1:1-4). Luke clearly states that he used materials given by eyewitnesses of the life of Christ.

In the Old Testament books of Kings and Chronicles, the writers often refer to other longer accounts of the lives of the kings. In 2 Kings 15, there are seven references to longer accounts in the "Book of Chronicles of the Kings of Israel" or Judah (2 Kings 15:6, 11, 15, 21, 26, 31, 36). This does *not* refer to the 1 and 2 Chronicles in the Bible but to ancient writings that no longer exist.

References to the "chronicles of Shemaiah the prophet and of Iddo the seer" appear in 2 Chronicles 12:15 and in several other places. The "book of the acts of Solomon" is mentioned in 1 Kings 11:41. These were obviously source materials for the writers of the biblical books of 1 and 2 Kings and 1 and 2 Chronicles.

The biblical writers did not always write with the precise accuracy demanded by scholarly writings of our day. They used approximations in time, distance, numbers. They used general identifications and popular descriptions familiar to their own times.

Guided by God, the biblical writers wrote in the forms and customary framework of their own time, just as we write in the forms and customary framework of our time. If they had not, their writings would have seemed very peculiar to the original readers.

When we examine the main purpose of the writers, we can see how careful and devoted they were to their purpose and how God guided their work so that it could be used through the centuries.

The four Gospel accounts of the life of Christ have frequent differences in detail. These differences give vitality and authenticity to the accounts. If four people witness an automobile accident, they will all describe it somewhat differently although the major details will probably be the same. The Gospel accounts of the life of Christ are like that, especially in regard to the last week before the crucifixion, which all four writers describe in some detail. The differences show that the information came from eyewitnesses and there was no effort by the early church to polish and harmonize the accounts as some have imagined.

In the light of what the biblical writers claim and what they do, it seems clear that inspiration involves God acting in the lives and words of His chosen servants in such a way that the Scriptures they wrote convey to readers what God wants us to know. In the Bible we have all that God chose to preserve so that we can know the infallible truth He conveyed to people of earlier generations.

After examining thousands of passages of Scripture, the authors of this book have concluded that the Bible teaches truth on all subjects it addresses in the ways and manners of expressing truth in ancient times. The Scriptures also illustrate truth by showing that error (idolatry, deceit, falsehood, and all forms of moral evil) brings tragedy.

The Bible Has Unity

The Bible is made up of sixty-six separate "books" that were written and edited over a period of approximately 1,400 years. What makes these sixty-six books hang together? Or do they? What unifies this vast quantity of material?

Several important basic themes unify the books of the Bible.

The Old and New Testaments emphasize the action of God as Creator. The subject of creation is multifaceted, but one idea comes through over and over: God has brought into existence all that is. He has made and continues to make what He wants for the purposes He has in mind.

We usually think of creation as the making of the universe and all living things. But creation is more than that. It also involves God's creative action in transforming a rebel into a disciple. This is part of God's current creative action.

Creation is also future. The future aspect gives meaning and unity to the Bible and to history (see Isa. 65:17; 2 Pet. 3:13; Rev. 21; 22). History begins and ends with creation when the final removal of sin and rebellion climaxes the "new creation."

The books of the Bible are drawn together by the pervasive action of God with His people Israel and with the rest of mankind. The theme of promise and fulfillment runs through Israel's history from the time that God spoke to Abraham and told him He would make of him a new nation (Gen. 12:2) until the birth of Jesus, the Messiah of Israel. God renewed His promises, gave new promises, clarified earlier promises, and fulfilled some promises. The theme of promise and fulfillment for Israel and the rest of mankind has continued since the coming of Christ.

The action of God in Christ unites the Bible. Christ's life and work had more meaning than was unfolded during His life on earth, for He Himself unified history and the Scriptures.

Christ gave meaning to all God's action in the past. Paul wrote, "But when the time had fully come, God sent forth his Son, born of woman, born under the law, to redeem those who were under the law, so that we might receive adoption as sons" (Gal. 4:4,5).

Christ also gave meaning to all that God would do in the future. He fulfilled Old Testament promises and came to make disciples of all nations. He made the concept of "the people of God" far broader than the Old Testament Hebrews understood. Emerging in the New Testament is the idea of the solidarity of the people of God in Christ.

Yet the actual working out of the concept of the broader people of God has come slowly through history. "There is neither Jew nor Greek, slave nor free, male nor female, for you are all one in Christ Jesus" (Gal. 3:28, *NIV*). This is Paul's pronouncement to the early church, and it was a revolutionary idea that has still not been truly activated.

Though distinctions between Jew and Gentile are said in the New Testament to be ended, anti-Semitism lives on. Slavery still exists in various economic and emotional forms. Sexual discrimination is still present. But these facts do not annul the unifying force of God's action in Christ. The Christian church ought to be a present sample of what will be when God's kingdom comes, when His will is done on earth as it is in heaven (Matt. 6:10).

The creative action of God among believers in Christ unifies the Bible. In the Old Testament, people were divided into two groups—Jews and Gentiles. But in the New Testament, a third group is created by God. Those who are joined to Christ (whether Jew or Gentile) are created into one new person (see Eph. 2:15). This third group is God's way of making peace between Jew and Gentile because both are transformed into something new and distinct—the church.

Much of the New Testament consists of letters written to churches, groups, or individual believers spread over a wide geographical area. They had different problems, different customs. But they were bound together with a living tie in the risen Christ. They were tied into one body, with one source of life—Christ, the head.

As Christians, they had been called to a new way of life that differed from the "old wine" of Judaism. The Holy Spirit worked within them, teaching, guiding, urging them to growth in the Body of Christ.

The Bible Has Diversity

The diversity of the Bible is almost as startling as its unity and contributes to the uniqueness of the Bible.

God's actions vary in His dealings with His people. We all go through life constantly surprised by what God does or does not do. God's dealings with the Apostle Paul furnish an example. Paul was imprisoned at various times in Jerusalem, Caesarea, and Rome. Each of his prison experiences was different, and so was God's action toward Paul different in these situations. God chose to use Paul's prison experiences so that he accomplished as much for the advance of the gospel in prison as outside prison.

People respond in diverse ways to God's leading. Sometimes the nation Israel governed itself, as in the days of the Judges and during the reigns of Saul, David, and Solomon. But after that period, Israel was often oppressed by foreign powers. The situations swung from one end of the pendulum to the other, and so did the response of the people.

During the reign of Josiah (640 to 609 BC) the nation prospered and worshiped God. The Israelites also prospered under Solomon, but during the latter part of his reign they began to turn away from God.

Sometimes God's judgment brought them to repentance, as in the time of Nehemiah (see Neh. 8).

Other times, as in the days of Jeremiah and Amos, the people responded to their prophets with hatred and resentment.

The purposes of the writers bring diversity. The Gospel of John is a much more theological interpretation of the life of Christ than is the Gospel of Mark. The differences in the outlook and purpose of the writers are easily perceived by the careful student.

God's messengers had varied and limited perspectives that made for diversity. When we seriously examine biblical teachings on such doctrines as the second coming of Christ, how and why believers are "elect," or teaching regarding baptism and the Lord's supper, we find differences in emphasis and interpretation by the writers of the Bible as well as by interpreters of the Bible through the centuries. Christians have had serious differences as to how various passages on the same subject should be integrated.

Most of us, in our most honest moments, confess that we do not have *all* the truth. We accept that (at least in theory) without too much discomfort. But it is also clear that none of God's inspired servants received *all* the truth. Paul said flatly, "For our knowledge is imperfect and our prophecy is imperfect; but when the perfect comes, the imperfect will pass away. . . . Now I know in part; then I shall understand fully, even as I have been fully understood (1 Cor. 13:9-12).

Each biblical writer or speaker has perspective intentionally limited by God. Each was given certain fragments of truth. Even if we could integrate perfectly all the fragments that God revealed to His servants in the Scriptures—a task of no mean proportions—the results would still be fragmentary.

Someday our limited perspective will be replaced

by full understanding. But since God Himself is the unifying force in the midst of diversity, we know that the diversity is just as important to God's purposes as the unity.

The Bible Tells Us About God

God did not give us the Bible to tickle our imaginations nor to give us grounds for profound theological debates. He gave us His Word—His revealing of Himself—so that we could know Him. That revelation culminated in the coming of Jesus Christ, the incarnate God. The Bible reveals God so that we can have a living relationship with the living God.

From the Bible we can learn what God intends for us to learn about Himself, ourselves, and our relationship with Him. It is the most important book ever written and it demands our closest attention and careful study if we are to see what God is actually saying to us. That is what sound biblical interpretation is all about.

The Bible is our guidebook in knowing God. "The unfolding of thy words gives light. . . . The sum of thy word is truth" (Ps. 119:130,160).

Questions for Discussion

1. In what ways does the Bible claim to be inspired?

2. The authors of *Understanding Scripture* say that the Bible is a "case study of people and their relationship to God." Can you think of examples of this and what we can learn from these "case studies"?

3. Why do you think books like Kings and Chronicles (that detail the history of the kings of Israel and Judah) are in the Bible? In what sense are these books a part of God's revelation to us?

The book of Esther does not mention the name of God. In what ways can it be a part of God's revelation?

4. Do you think all sixty-six books of the Bible are equally "the word of God"? Why or why not?

5. Do you think all parts of the Bible are equally important to us? Why or why not?

Chapter 4

What to Look for in Bible Translations

It is not easy to translate ideas from one language to another. A good translator must be master both of the original language and of the language into which he is translating. Most of us struggle to find the right words in our native language to express the feeling, idea, or fact we want to communicate. And often our words are misunderstood by those who hear or read them. "Yes, that is what I said (or wrote), but you are misunderstanding what I meant by that." Most of us have said that or had it said to us. Communication is difficult even under ideal circumstances.

One reason communication is hard is that our tone of voice or the look on our face as we speak often reveals more than the actual words we use. In writing, of course, we do not have a tone of voice or a facial expression, but we have subtle nuances in the way we phrase things. Someone who translates this to another language must try to capture those nuances, rephrase them in the idiom of another language and still communicate those important shades of meaning. Because this is so difficult, translations often give the nuances of the translator rather than those of the original writer or speaker.

The Bible's Three Languages

Each of the three languages in which the Bible was originally written—Aramaic, Hebrew, and koine Greek—involves specific problems for the translator.

Aramaic was used in almost six chapters of Daniel, in all or parts of four chapters of Ezra and in one verse in Jeremiah (10:11) and one verse in Genesis (31:47). The Aramaic language has been dead for many centuries. To understand the meaning of the words and the grammar and sentence structure of this language, translators must depend on ancient secular manuscripts such as the Elephantine Papyri, consisting of letters, contracts and community happenings.

Fortunately, the sections of Aramaic in the Bible are short, and it is a kind of first-cousin language to Hebrew. It is an important language, for it was the everyday language of Jewish people in Palestine from 350 BC up through and including the time of Christ. It was no doubt the native tongue of Jesus and the apostles.

Hebrew, in which most of the Old Testament was written, died as a spoken language about 300 BC. It has been revived, however, in modern Israel. Although modern Hebrew was based on ancient Hebrew, it has already changed considerably because so many new words had to be added in keeping with modern times and culture. This is not surprising, for language is always dynamic—constantly changing and developing. Even the Hebrew of the early part of the Old Testament (Genesis, Job) is not the same as that written in the later books such as Nehemiah and Ezra.

Koine Greek, the language in which the New Testament was written, represents a certain period in the development of the Greek language. Like many other languages, modern Greek has flattened out—become simpler, with fewer cases of nouns, fewer moods of verbs. New Testament Greek is quite different from modern Greek.

Mastery of biblical languages requires a lifetime of study. Many fine scholars have given their lives to such study and every student of the Bible has profited from their work.

Most Christians know little about biblical languages nor will they ever become masters of them. But all of us can become aware of the problems involved in language and the limitations these place on us. We will then be less likely to make the kinds of errors in interpreting the Bible that arise easily from attaching undue emphasis to questionable words, or having some important belief rest on a few selected verses.

Biblical Languages Were More Oral than Written

All of the Bible was written many centuries before the invention of the printing press. The biblical languages (Hebrew, Aramaic, and Greek) were spoken much more than they were written. Most people could not read or write, so nearly all communication was in speech. History, facts, and stories were handed down orally from one generation to another. To such people the spoken word was much more important than it is to us.

On the occasions when ancient Hebrew and Aramaic were written, words were written without vowels. For this reason, the actual sounds and pronunciations of Hebrew and Aramaic words are surrounded by some mystery. Only the consonants were written and the exact word had to be determined by the context.

It is not always easy to determine the vowels from the context. If this principle were applied to English, the words farm, firm, from, frame, form and forum would all be written "frm." It could be difficult to determine the correct words from the context. A sentence reading, "He chose the frm" might mean he chose the farm or the frame or the forum or the firm.

Between AD 500 and 600—centuries after Hebrew had died as a spoken language, a group of people known as the Masoretic scholars decided that something should be done to preserve the pronunciation of the Hebrew words. The Hebrew text had been handed down through centuries by hand copying and it was written with only the consonant sounds. The Masoretic scholars now added "vowel points" to the Hebrew words. By placing a point or dot at a certain position above or below or within the consonant letters, the scholars indicated which vowels they thought belonged in the words. This has become known as the Masoretic text. While it is helpful, it is by no means indisputable. After all, the Masoretic scholars had no way of being sure whether a combination of letters like "frm" meant farm, forum, or firm, if the context did not make it clear.

In the Old Testament there are many passages where the original meaning is not sure. For example, in Hebrews 11:21, the New Testament writers described Jacob's death this way: "By faith Jacob, when dying, blessed each of the sons of Joseph, bowing in worship over the head of his *staff*" (italics added). But our Genesis account of this story in 47:31 reads: "Then Israel bowed himself upon the head of his *bed*" (italics added).

Why the difference? The Hebrew text has the equivalent of the letters MTTH. The translators of the Old Testament version used by the writer of Hebrews (the Septuagint) thought the vowels should be added to form the word *matteh*, meaning staff or rod. Those who prepared the later Masoretic text, and other more recent Hebrew scholars, believed the vowels should be those in the word *mittah*, which means couch or bed. So our Genesis account in English reads "bed" but the Hebrews account reads "staff."

Hebrew and Greek Were Rich Languages

Hebrew is a rich language—Greek even more so. The vocabularies of these languages were so extensive that they permitted fine delineations of meaning, and the grammar and syntax were capable of expressing delicate differences. English often cannot do this. Therefore the English language sometimes cannot show all that the biblical languages expressed.

Sometimes these language differences can be just enough to convey erroneous ideas. For example, in English we cannot differentiate between *you* singular and *you* plural. In our highly individualistic society, we tend to read every *you* as referring to an individual. But in the Scripture, written in a culture that stressed group solidarity, the *you* is often plural.

Philippians 1:6 reads: "I am sure that he who began a good work in you will bring it to completion at the day of Jesus Christ." We usually read this verse as an individual promise that "he who began a good work in *me* . . ." But the Greek text shows that the *you* in this case is plural. It refers to a group—the church at Philippi. Now the meaning changes from a promise to the individual to a promise that his church will prevail. "He who began a good work among *you* [plural] will keep on working until its completion in the day of Jesus Christ."

How can we know whether *you* is singular or plural in the Greek? One way is to consult a good commentary. (See the bibliography at the end of this book for a list of helpful commentaries.) Differences can sometimes be seen by consulting other versions where the translator may have rearranged the sentence to make clear whether the word is singular or plural.

Sometimes a careful study of the context shows whether the writer is thinking of *you* singular or *you* plural. Actually, this is true of Philippians 1:6, but we often do not study whole passages in context as we should.

The verbs in the biblical languages give greater depth of meaning than do our English verbs. The Greek has an aorist tense that expresses totality or wholeness of action. Greek also has perfect tenses that describe action as a state (in the past, present, or future), a permanent effect of action. Greek has present and imperfect tenses that describe action as *continuous*.

Although English has compound tenses (i.e., he is believing, he has believed) they are not used as freely as their Greek equivalents, and translators must often surrender the fine distinctions in the effort to make a translation highly readable and in keeping with our idiomatic language.

A literal translation of 1 Corinthians 1:18 would read, "For the word of the cross is to those who are in the process of perishing, foolishness; but to us who

are in the process of being saved, the power of God."
The verb in the Greek is the present participle. This
is awkward and difficult to convey in English. The
King James translators said, "For the preaching of
the cross is to them that perish foolishness; but unto
us which are saved it is the power of God." The process idea is quite lost in that translation. The
Revised Standard Version does better by saying,
"who are perishing" and "who are being saved" but
even then the full force of the process idea does not
come through. Perhaps the *New English Bible* comes
closer by saying, "on their way to ruin" and "on the
way to salvation."

Most lay students of the Bible cannot master
enough Greek or Hebrew to make use of the fine lines
of meaning in these languages, but we can realize our
limitations because of this and refrain from pro-
nouncements based on a pronoun or past tense or on
English grammatical constructions that may be
unable to express the full force of the original language.

On the other hand, there are some instances in
which Greek is less precise than English. This introduces other problems.

The current discussions about biblical teachings
on the role of women in the church and society is
complicated by the fact that Greek uses the same
word *gune* for "woman" and for "wife" and the word
aner means either "man" or "husband."

For example, 1 Corinthians 11:3 reads "the head
of the *gune* is the *aner*." This passage introduces a
discussion about how men and women are to pray
and prophesy in public gatherings. Paul suggests a
difference in head covering or hairstyle.[1] Should the
Greek word *gune* in "the head of *gune* is *aner*" be

translated woman or wife? And should *aner* be translated husband or man? The meaning of the passage is quite different, depending on how the words are translated. King James uses woman and man. *RSV*, strangely, uses "woman" and "husband," using marital status in one and not in the other! *The Living Bible* and *Today's English Version* use wife and husband. Most other versions agree with King James and use woman and man.

We believe it should be woman and man because the rest of the chapter does not discuss wives and husbands but rather how men and women should pray and prophesy in public gatherings. This is a clear instance of the translator being forced to make a choice in what he thinks the Apostle Paul meant. Such a passage that is so obviously open to varying meanings should never be basic to any important teaching.

This situation appears also in 1 Timothy 3:8-13 where there is a discussion about qualifications for deacons. In the middle of the paragraph, verse 11 reads, "the women [*gune*] likewise must be serious, no slanderers, but temperate, faithful in all things." The King James translated it, "Even so must their *wives* be . . ." The word *gune* that appears here does not tell us whether Paul meant wives, women in general, or women deacons. The only guide to meaning in this case must be the context, and the differences between translations indicate that biblical scholars do not agree as to what Paul had in mind.

Style of Ancient Writings

Original writings of the Bible and early copies of them were written in ancient style. That meant there were no spaces between words, no punctuation, no paragraphs, no capitals and small letters. Everything was in the equivalent of capital letters.

Although lack of space between words may not seem serious, it could make a drastic difference. Consider the sentence: GODISNOWHERE. That could mean "God is now here" or it could mean "God is nowhere"!

Imagine a line from Romans 3:23 written in the style of biblical Greek manuscripts. The English equivalent might look something like this: FORALL-HAVESINNEDANDCOMESHORTOFTHEGLORYOF-GOD. If that looks difficult, imagine how it would look written in the Hebrew style without vowels: FR-LLHVSNNDNDCMSHRTFTHGLRYFGD. Of course, Hebrew letters are very different from our letters and they also read from right to left!

Those who translated from the earliest manuscripts had to decide where the word divisions came, where sentences began and ended, where to put periods and commas, and what were direct quotations.

The decisions were often difficult, and the differences of opinion show up among the translations. If 1 Corinthians 14:33,34 were written with word divisions but with no punctuation it would read: For God is not a God of confusion but of peace as in all the churches of the saints the women should keep silence in the churches for they are not permitted to speak but should be subordinate as even the law says.

Even the punctuation makes a difference in meaning. Does the phrase, "as in all the churches of the saints" belong with the sentence that comes before it: "God is not a God of confusion but of peace"? Or does it belong with the sentence that follows it: "the women should keep silence . . ."? Translators differ as to where to put the period and where to start a new sentence.

Divisions into chapters and verses were not added until the Middle Ages. These divisions make it easier for us to find passages in the Bible, but they may also make us think that the writer arranged his thoughts in the same groupings that appear in our Bibles. That may or may not be true.

Some are clearly wrong. First Corinthians 11:1 so clearly belongs at the end of chapter 10 that several translations (including the *RSV*) simply show that verse as the last sentence in the paragraph that closes chapter 10.

Some translations, like the *King James Version*, have no paragraphs at all, but treat each verse as a separate entity. This easily confuses the reader who often does not realize that the verses and chapters were not a part of the original text.

New Testament Quotations of the Old Testament May Be Different

Serious Bible students soon learn that New Testament writers frequently quote the Old Testament. If the student looks up the Old Testament reference (usually indicated by a marginal note) he or she may find that the Old Testament text is quite different from the quotation in the New Testament.

Hebrews 12:6 quotes Proverbs 3:12 like this: "For the Lord disciplines him whom he loves, and chastises every son whom he receives." But if we look up Proverbs 3:12 in the Old Testament, we find that it actually says, "For the Lord reproves him whom he loves, as a father the son in whom he delights." Why the difference?

The Hebrews 12:6 quotation, like the majority of

the New Testament quotations, is from the Septuagint translation of the Old Testament. This was a Greek translation of the Old Testament made between 250 and 150 BC for the benefit of Greek-speaking Jews.

During this period of Greek supremacy, many Jews left Palestine and settled in countries around the Mediterranean where Greek was the everyday language. Many Jews who grew up in these areas never learned Hebrew and could not read the Hebrew Old Testament. They needed the Old Testament in the Greek language that they now spoke. The early church grew mostly among these Greek-speaking Jews and among Greek-speaking Gentiles. The Septuagint became the Bible of the dispersed Jews and of the early church, made up of Greek-speaking Gentile converts and Greek-speaking converts from Judaism.

The writer of Hebrews used the Septuagint when he quoted Proverbs in his letter. This is another case where the translators of the Septuagint differed from later translators in the choice of vowels for a Hebrew word. Septuagint translators chose vowels that made a Hebrew word meaning "he causes pain." Modern translators believed the word made better sense with vowels that meant "as a father."

The writer of the Epistle to the Hebrews always quotes from the Septuagint, indicating that he may not have known the Hebrew version. Even Paul often used the Septuagint (although he knew Hebrew). In fact, fifty-one of the ninety-three Old Testament quotations Paul uses in his letters are from the Septuagint even though he also knew the Hebrew text. He realized that most of his readers knew Greek but not Hebrew. Quotations from the Septuagint explain many of the differences between our Old Testament readings and the way passages are quoted in the New Testament.

Jesus spoke and taught in Aramaic. The New Testament Gospels that tell about the life and words of Jesus were written originally in Greek. However, the common language of the people in Palestine among whom Jesus lived was not Greek but Aramaic—a sort of first cousin to Hebrew. Greek was the language of commerce. Jesus was undoubtedly bilingual and He probably also knew Hebrew from His study in synagogue schools. But we can be sure that Jesus spoke Aramaic as He walked along the roads and taught the people who gathered around Him. Aramaic was their "language of the heart"—that which they used around their own tables and in which they could communicate most intimately and deeply.

The words of Jesus as they were originally recorded in Greek by Matthew, Mark, Luke and John were *translations of what Jesus actually said in Aramaic.* The sayings of Jesus no doubt circulated orally, both in Aramaic and in Greek, for the fifteen to thirty years before any of the Gospels were written. This may account for some of the differences among the Gospel accounts, for translations by nature allow for more than one possible way of expressing an idea.

The nature of languages and of the problems involved in handing down writings over a period of thousands of years, and the process of translating from one language to another are all highly complex.

How to Judge a Translation
Today, with so many Bible translations from which to choose, how can the honest Bible student know which one is best? The answer is not easy.

There are two major types of translations. Each has its advantages and weaknesses.

Committee translations. Committee translations are done by groups of scholars who work together on certain books or sections of the Bible and who are usually specialists in Greek, Hebrew, or Aramaic and are knowledgeable about the history and culture of the book they are translating. Examples of committee translations are *King James Version*, *Revised Standard Version*, *New International Version*, and the *New English Bible* (done by British scholars).

The interaction of well-trained scholars on a translation often weeds out the gross inaccuracies and renderings that are strongly influenced by the personal doctrines or prejudices of individual members of the committee.

On the other hand, group translations usually lack the literary style and flair that contributes to the readability of one-person paraphrases.

One-person paraphrases. These are produced basically by one person who is skilled in literary style. Such persons may or may not be skilled in biblical languages, but they often have scholars as consultants to advise them on difficult passages. Examples of such translations are Ken Taylor's *The Living Bible*; Robert Bratcher's *Good News for Modern Man* (also known as *Today's English Version*); and J. B. Phillips' *New Testament in Modern English*.

The one-person translations usually have greater literary flair and a more consistent style than the committee translations. They are basically easier to read. Their weakness is that they often reflect the doctrinal and social framework of the translator and sometimes add to or subtract from the actual text.

For example, 1 Corinthians 11:10 actually says in

the Greek text, "Because of this, a woman ought to have authority upon the head because of the angels." All of the committee translations mentioned above stay fairly close to this literal translation. However, all three of the one-man paraphrases add to the text the interpretations of the translator as to the meaning of the actual words:

The Living Bible: "So a woman should wear a covering on her head as a sign that she is under man's authority, a fact for all the angels to notice and rejoice in."

Good News for Modern Man: "On account of the angels, then, a woman should have a covering over her head to show that she is under her husband's authority."

New Testament in Modern English: "For this reason a woman ought to bear on her head an outward sign of man's authority for all the angels to see."

The Greek text says nothing about men or husbands. Those additions are the translators' interpretations of what they think the text means. Their interpretations may or may not be right, but they have moved beyond the actual text to their interpretation of the text.

Which of the committee translations are best? The *King James Version* was an excellent translation in 1611 when it was completed. However, the ancient manuscripts on which it was based were few in number and questionable in quality. Many new and better ancient manuscripts have been found since that time (including the Dead Sea Scrolls) which have been used by the more recent committee translations. While no translations are perfect, the *RSV* and *NIV* are probably among the better of the committee translations available today.

While the one-person paraphrases often have an exciting sense of vitality and may throw new light on familiar passages, serious students should always compare the paraphrases with one or more committee translations. If an idea appears in a one-man translation that does not appear in most committee translations, it is a tip that the idea may represent an interpretation of the translator. For this reason, paraphrases should not be used for serious Bible study unless they are compared with committee translations.

As translators become more sensitive to their own biases, and as additional older and better biblical manuscripts are found, Bible translations will probably improve further. Meanwhile we can be thankful for the ones we have and recognize that, in spite of their human limitations, they can and do convey God's message to us.

Questions for Discussion

1. The original manuscripts of the Bible had no chapters or verses. Chapters and verses were added to our Bibles a few hundred years ago.

Do the chapter and verse divisions make a difference in the way you read your Bible? Do you think they are a help or a hindrance?

2. The Hebrew text was originally written with consonants only—no vowels. To see how difficult this is to read, try the following experiment.

Assume you want to tell something to the person sitting next to you. Write it down on a piece of paper. (Make it something very simple and write no more than ten or twelve words.) Now, instead of giving that to your neighbor, write it again, this time all in capital letters, without punctuation, no spaces between words, and omit all vowels—AEIOUY. Copy it on a separate piece of paper and hand it to your neighbor. See how quickly (if ever!) the person can figure out what you wrote.

3. If you understand something about language problems in the Bible, will it make any difference in the way you interpret the Bible?

Note

1. The Greek text does not clarify what Paul means. The literal words are "down from the head." The word "veil" never appears in 1 Corinthians 11 although several translations use the word "veil" where Paul writes "down from the head." Paul may have been writing about a veil, or he may have been referring to a particular long hairstyle. Since the passage mentions hair length several times (see 1 Cor. 11:5,6,13,14,15), we think he was writing about a hairstyle as a covering.

Chapter 5

How the Bible Was Written and Compiled

The Protestant Bible is a collection of sixty-six books—thirty-nine in the Old Testament and twenty-seven in the New Testament. The Roman Catholic Bible has the same New Testament books as the Protestant, but has an additional twelve books in the Old Testament.

These books were written by many different people over a period of more than one thousand years.

The Bible is known as the *canon* for the Christian faith. *Canon* means a collection of books or writings accepted by a group of people as the basis for their beliefs and how they should live and worship. Almost all major religions (and some minor ones) have a canon. Muslims, Hindus, Mormons, Buddhists—all have their own canons.

The Old Testament is the canon for Judaism. The Old and New Testaments form the canon for Christianity. How were our sixty-six books—written over such a long period of time—brought together to form our canonical Bible?

Misunderstandings are common about this subject. God did *not* in a supernatural way inform Moses or Paul or Luke that what they were writing was or would become a part of the canon for Christianity. Nor did a group of church leaders or a church council "choose" what should be in the Bible. Actually, the canon was established in a process that took between fifty and 250 years for the New Testament and probably even longer for the Old Testament.

If we trace the canonization of the New Testament writings we can get a glimpse of the actual process. We know that the books of the New Testament were probably written between AD 50 and 100. Precise dates are not established for all the books.

There is evidence that at least some of the writings of the Apostle Paul were collected *as a group* about AD 90. We know this through the study of textual criticism—how the books of the Bible were physically copied and handed down through the centuries before the invention of the printing press. Before the printing press, manuscripts had to be copied by hand. Often one person copied by hand a manuscript that had been copied by someone else before him. Other times one person read and a group of scribes all wrote what was dictated to them. Different individuals and groups had certain ways of copying that were different from other persons or groups.

The study of groups of old manuscripts of Paul's letters shows that the textual variants are the same in one letter of Paul as in another. This shows that they were copied as a group of letters rather than individually. The scribes had certain habits of writing and transcribing and the similarities show that the same scribes copied these letters at the same time.

Ignatius, an early church father, wrote several letters (that have been preserved) between AD 95 and 110 in which he quoted from Paul's epistles. Ignatius wrote to some of the same churches that Paul wrote to. When Ignatius quoted Paul it indicated that he knew Paul's writings and that Paul's writings were considered authoritative among the readers.

The four Gospels in the New Testament form an interesting study in canon development. All four Gospels are mentioned by various church fathers beginning in AD 90. However, between AD 100 and 140 a number of other writings about the life of Christ (known as apocryphal gospels) were circulated. Many of these were produced by a sect known as the gnostics. The gnostics believed that Christ was entirely divine, but that He was not truly human. They believed that the *divine Christ* came upon the *man Jesus* at His baptism and left Him at the crucifixion. In order to support that view, they had to rewrite many of the sayings in the four Gospels.

Marcion was a gnostic, or at least held views similar to those of the gnostics. His sect flourished between AD 130 and 155. Marcion believed that the God of the Old Testament was not the God of Jesus Christ. For this reason, he repudiated the Old Testament. He then had to create a canon of his own to take the place of the Old Testament (which was largely the Bible of the early church). In Marcion's canon he included ten letters of Paul and the Gospel of Luke. Marcion's strong influence forced the early church to declare that our *four* Gospels were all sacred, authoritative writings (canonical) and that the gnostic gospels being written should not be used for readings in the church.

For at least partly the same reason, the church by

AD 150 was acknowledging that the letters of Paul were authoritative.

In 1740, a medieval librarian found a list of sacred writings in a library near Milan, Italy. The list has been dated between AD 190 and 210 and includes twenty-two of the twenty-seven books in our New Testament. It includes the four Gospels, thirteen letters of Paul, Acts, Jude, 1 and 2 John, and Revelation. It omits Hebrews, 3 John, 1 and 2 Peter, and James. It includes two books *not* included in our canon—the Wisdom of Solomon and the Apocalypse of Peter. By this time strong consensus was developing but there were still some differences of opinion.

Several factors influenced the early church in recognizing a writing as canonical:

It was written by an apostle or someone acquainted with an apostle.

It was widely used in public worship.

It showed a fresh treatment of Christian truth and faith.

Four church fathers were particularly important in recognizing the New Testament writings as authoritative. They were Irenaeus (AD 130 to 202); Tertullian (AD 160 to 220); Origen (AD 185 to 254), and Eusebius of Caesarea (AD 260 to 340). Writings of Eusebius which have been handed down show that he worked out categories of books that were "acknowledged" as authoritative or "disputed."

The process of recognizing which books of the New Testament were authoritative took place over a period of 250 years and involved the whole church—Christians in Rome, Constantinople, Alexandria (Egypt) and Greece. Some parts of the church took longer to recognize writings than other parts. God did not magically give everyone the same list. Rather, the Spirit of God worked among Christian groups wherever they were, primarily through their use of the writings, to indicate that these particular books were authentic statements about the gospel and were authoritative for all Christians.

This process took place during a time of intense persecution. From the time of Nero (AD 64) to the time of Constantine (311) the church faced wave after wave of extreme persecution. Thousands of Christians were put to death for their faith. During periods of such persecution, Christians were sometimes asked to surrender authoritative books of faith. Obviously the church by this time knew which books were to be safeguarded. Those who did surrender such books were later ostracized by the church after the persecution stopped.

The list of authoritative New Testament books was apparently established before 367, for in a letter written that year by Athanasius, bishop of Alexandria, he lists the same twenty-seven books as those now accepted in our New Testament. The same list is clearly stated in the Council of Chalcedon in 451.

At the time of the Reformation there was no disagreement between the Roman Catholic church, the Eastern Orthodox church or the Protestant reformers as to the books that belonged in the New Testament.

The Old Testament Canon

To establish the canon of the Old Testament was more difficult and there still remains a difference of opinion between the Protestant and the Roman Catholic branches of Christendom on this matter. The Protestant churches follow the canon apparently accepted by the Palestinian Jews before the time of

Christ; while the Roman Catholic Old Testament includes twelve additional books.

The Jewish historian Josephus lived between AD 37 and 100. In his writings, there is a list of Old Testament books that probably is the same as the books in the Protestant Old Testament. We say "probably" because the material was arranged and put together differently, so that there were only twenty-two books. For example, Ruth was included with Judges, and Lamentations with Jeremiah.

There seems to have been three steps in recognizing which books of the Old Testament belonged in the canon.

1. Composition. The *words* of the Old Testament prophets were recognized as the authoritative word of God when they were first declared *orally*. They were also recognized as authoritative when they were written down.

2. Recognition and re-recognition of the canon. As the writings of the prophets and others were handed down, they had to be recognized continuously as authoritative. They otherwise would not have been copied and recopied for succeeding generations. In the Old Testament books of Kings and Chronicles, many other writings are mentioned such as "the book of Shemaiah the prophet and of Iddo the seer" (see 2 Chron. 12:15 and 2 Chron. 13:22), but these were not preserved.

3. Final recognition of the canon. Evidence that some Old Testament books were considered authoritative come in writings that appeared between 500 BC and the time of Christ.

About 432 BC, Nehemiah expelled from the Jewish colony at Jerusalem some of the Jews who had intermarried with foreign women. Those expelled became the community of Samaritans. This group used the Pentateuch only (the first five books of the Old Testament). This was apparently one part of the Old Testament that the Samaritans clearly recognized as authoritative. Whether the other Jews in Jerusalem recognized other parts of the Old Testament as authoritative at that time, we have no way of knowing. Nehemiah 8:1 speaks of Ezra bringing "the book of the law of Moses which the Lord had given to Israel." This refers to the Pentateuch and shows clearly that it was acknowledged as sacred.

Between 250 and 150 BC, the Old Testament was translated into Greek in Alexandria, Egypt. This is known as the Septuagint version. It is the earliest translation of the Old Testament—in fact, it is the earliest known translation of *any* literature from one language to another! The Septuagint includes all thirty-nine books of the Protestant Old Testament, plus the twelve additional books (known as the apocrypha) that appear in the Roman Catholic Old Testament, plus three additional books that appeared in Jerome's Latin Vulgate translation. The Septuagint includes additional material beyond these. It was really a Greek translation of important religious writings—a kind of "religious library of important materials." Whether the Alexandrians considered all the writings in the Septuagint to be authoritative, we have no way of knowing.

Some evidence seems to indicate that the Alexandrians did not consider all the writings in the Septuagint to be equally authoritative. Philo, the famous Jewish theologian of Alexandria, lived between 30 BC and AD 50. He often quoted the Septuagint Old Testament in his writings but never quoted the apocryphal books as Scripture.

The Talmud is a collection of Jewish stories, teachings, traditions, comments about and interpretations of the Old Testament. It was gathered and written down between AD 250 and 550. The Talmud refers only to the writings in the thirty-nine books of the Old Testament—not to the apocryphal books of the Septuagint.

From the time of Saint Jerome (AD 340 to 420) to the time of Martin Luther (1483 to 1546), the apocryphal books were recognized as valuable for study by Christians but were not considered to be on the same level as the thirty-nine books of the Old Testament.

Thus it is apparent that Jews and Christians (both Protestant and Roman Catholic) agree that the thirty-nine books of the Old Testament are canonical. The only differences revolve around the twelve additional books that appear in the Roman Catholic Old Testament.

Questions for Discussion

1. Most of the terms used in this chapter, that describe how our Bible was compiled, are familiar to us. The authors describe these terms for you. How many do you remember or understand?

    a. canon   c. Talmud

    b. Septuagint   d. apocrypha

2. Who were the following people and what value is there in recognizing them?

    a. Ignatius   b. Josephus

3. Does it disturb you to hear that "God did *not* in a supernatural way inform Moses or Paul or Luke that what they were writing was or would become a part of the canon of Christianity"? Why or why not?

Chapter 6

The Life and Times of Bible People

No event occurs in a vacuum. Every person lives within a cultural and historical situation and is strongly influenced by it. Every biblical event and teaching arose from and is part of a particular history and culture.

In one sense, history is what actually happened in a certain period of time. However, the history we know is actually the historian's *selection* of facts in the life of an individual, group, nation or group of nations. The historian selects facts as he or she tries to see meaning in the acts and purposes of the person or nation. Thus all history, written or oral, is inherently an interpretation of events by the historian, regardless of how objective and honest the historian is trying to be. It cannot be otherwise.

History, as conceived by historians, is people-centered and event-centered. It is the account of persons and events and their effects on the lives and events that followed.

But Christians believe that history is more than

this—it is the unfolding of God's plan or purpose. The Christian cannot center history exclusively on people or events and ignore God and His acts.

The Bible involves a great deal of history. But in the Scripture the actions of people and the actions of God are recorded together. In this kind of history, people meet God in a God-ordained sequence of experiences in which they may become estranged and hostile to God, or they may be reconciled to God. There is no division between secular and sacred history.

Most portions of the Bible are more readily understood when we set them against their own historical and cultural situations. Only then can we begin to understand why people thought and acted as they did. Only then are we ready to move to the next step of understanding the meaning of Bible events and teachings for our day.

Study Historical and Cultural Backgrounds

Sometimes historical and cultural backgrounds of biblical writings are hard to determine. Biblical scholars often disagree as to the date of writing of certain books. For example, the book of Obadiah has been dated as early as 900 BC and as late as 400 BC. If scholars have a hard time determining when it was written, how can the average Bible student know anything about the historical and cultural background of the book?

Fortunately, the situation is not as hopeless as might first appear. There *is* general consensus among biblical scholars as to the dates of many books of the Bible. Variations as wide as that of Obadiah are the exception rather than the rule.

But even with Obadiah we are not left in a void, for

the historical *situation* is more important than the precise historical *date*. The contents of Obadiah show that it was written at a time of conflict between the descendants of Esau and the descendants of Jacob, his brother. Whether the conflict occurred in the ninth century BC or the sixth century BC or some other century makes little difference in understanding the vision of Obadiah.

With regard to historical dating we must point out that biblical scholars often have prejudices that tend to control their thinking about the time certain books were written. For example, some scholars are convinced, because of their own theological views, that God never revealed the future to his prophets. This, of course, makes predictive prophecy impossible. Therefore, *because of their theological views*, such interpreters will date a book containing prophecy at a time *after* the prophesied event took place. The interpreter may then insist that prophecy is just another way of writing history.

A German phrase, *Sitz im Leben*, has become almost a part of the English language among those who investigate historical backgrounds. It means "life situation," and includes the history and culture of the individual or group or nation being studied.

Another part of the biblical picture is equally important. It is known as *Sitz im Glauben* or "faith situation." It inquires about the relationship of the person or nation to God. Both the "life situation" and the "faith situation" are important in understanding any section of the Bible. But where can we find such information?

Use an Atlas, Dictionary and Commentary
A good Bible atlas or a Bible dictionary gives some

geographical, political, and cultural information. A good commentary supplies historical information of the "life and faith" situation of the passage being studied. These are essential if we are to make the right leap from what the passage meant to the first readers to what it means for us today.

For example, a commentary on Paul's letters to the Corinthians should show in nearly every passage the situation of Paul's original readers. The questions the Corinthians were asking Paul to answer came straight from their own "life and faith" situations. Christianity came to Corinth, a city with a long history and distinct cultural patterns. Only when these are understood will the reader see the significance of Paul's statements on marriage (1 Cor. 7), on conduct in public meetings (1 Cor. 11 and 14), on separation from idolatry (1 Cor. 8:4-13), and on several other subjects.

Know the geography of the ancient world. Palestine was the crossroads of the Near East. Through this land marched the great leaders of world empires. To the Jews, Palestine was THE LAND that God had promised them (see Gen. 35:12; Heb. 11:9). The modern Jew, who is often quite irreligious, shares with his devoutly religious ancestors a passionate devotion to THE LAND. In fact, the land has become almost an idol taking the place of God. Many atheistic and agnostic Jews are still ardent Zionists. To the Christian the land is important as the place where God performed many of His mighty acts.

Understand political settings and backgrounds. Political rulers played an important role in the life of the nation Israel and were an influence on the early church. Rulers and their attitudes throw light on Scripture passages.

At the time of the birth of Christ, Palestine was ruled by Roman procurators or governors. The Jews hated the Romans and the Romans hated the Jews— both with good reason! Both sides had tried intermittently to irritate the other and to get along together. Antagonisms were running deep at the time of the birth of Christ and war between the two sides was only a question of time. In this setting of suspicion and distrust, Jesus was born, lived, was put to death, and rose again. In this same atmosphere, the good news of the gospel spread across Palestine, Asia Minor, Greece and Italy. Early Christianity did not have ideal political surroundings.

The serious Bible student needs to know the political history behind specific incidents. The Samaritan woman with whom Jesus talked at the well of Sychar came from a history of 500 years of political conflict with the Jews. This history of antagonism colored her feelings. Her remarks and the statement, "Now Jews do not associate on friendly terms with Samaritans" (*AT*) in John 4:9 show that animosity was the accepted way of life—just as animosity today is part of the way of life between Jews and Arabs.

Know as much as possible about the culture of people of Bible times. Culture involves the habits, customs, tools, institutions, arts, music, and literary productions of any people—everything they create and use. The kind of homes people live in, their tools, clothing, food, means of travel are sometimes significant in understanding the Bible.

In the story of Jesus healing the paralytic man, the accounts say that because of the crowds, four men went up on a roof, opened a hole and let the sick man down in front of Jesus (see Matt. 9:1-8; Mark 2:1-12; Luke 5:17-26).

If the reader visualizes an American ranch-type home or a two-story colonial, the idea of tearing up the roof and letting the man down through a hole envisions scenes of destruction and a shower of falling plaster. But when we understand that a Palestinian home had a flat roof covered by adobe tiles, we can see how this incident was possible. The four friends carried the paralytic man up the outside stairs (every house had such stairs) to the flat roof. At the place on the roof where they were directly over Jesus, the friends removed some of "the tiles" (Luke 5:19) and let the man down through the opening in front of Jesus. It was a simple matter to then replace the tiles. With the proper background information the story of the paralytic and his four friends who had faith becomes alive and thrilling.

Leonardo da Vinci's portrait of the Last Supper, although a masterpiece in its portrayal of the twelve apostles and Christ, has helped establish in our minds an erroneous cultural picture that makes the events of that evening hard to understand. Instead of sitting upright at a long table, as in da Vinci's painting, the Jews of that time (like the Greeks) usually ate in a reclining position. The table for the Last Supper was probably U-shaped, with Jesus at the curve of the U. As the disciples and Jesus reclined on their couches around the table, Jesus spoke of His betrayal. John 13:23 records, "One of his disciples, whom Jesus loved, was lying close to the breast of Jesus." The Gospel then recounts what is obviously a private conversation between that disciple and Jesus. Knowing the customs we can now visualize the Last Supper with men lying on couches so that the head of one man would be close to the breast of the man on his right.

Later that evening, Jesus dipped a morsel into a dish and "gave it to Judas" (John 13:26). To us, having one person dip something into a dish (*KJV* says, "dipped the sop") and hand it to someone else to eat is repulsive. But within Jewish culture it was a symbol of deep friendship. The act of Jesus now becomes moving and significant.

Know the socio-religious customs of Bible people. In every culture, much of life is determined by socio-religious customs. Birth, marriage, and death are nearly always surrounded by socio-religious ceremonies. This was true of the Jews, and their patterns play an important part in understanding the Bible.

After Jesus was born, His parents observed three customary religious ceremonies: (1) Jesus' circumcision on the eighth day after His birth when He was named Jesus (Luke 2:21; see also Lev. 12:3); (2) Mary's purification, according to the law, thirty-three days later (Lev. 12:4-7); and at the same time, (3) Jesus' dedication (Luke 2:22-39).

Understanding customs in Old Testament stories clarifies phrases that would otherwise sound strange. Legal transactions in ancient times often took place at the gate of the city. When we read in the book of Esther that Mordecai is "sitting at the king's gate" (Esther 2:19), we know that he was one of the judges of his day. His office was at the king's gate.

Try to understand the economy of people in Bible times. Decisions people made were often influenced by their economy. Absence of rainfall meant famine. Earthquakes blotted out whole cities.

In time of war, conquerors often deported the leaders of vanquished people. They also sent the more skilled workmen to some other country, leaving largely the poor and elderly who could not lead or organize a rebellion against the conqueror. The deported people were not prisoners in their new land. They could and did build homes and establish businesses, but such exiles could not return to their homeland. The conquerors often sent many of their own people to settle in the conquered land and to become the new political leaders.

When the Assyrians conquered the Northern Kingdom (Israel) in 722 BC, many of the Israelites were deported. Most of them never returned and were eventually assimilated into the population where they lived. They became the "ten lost tribes of Israel."

When the Southern Kingdom (Judah) fell to Babylon in 586 BC, many of the Jews were deported. When Cyrus, the Persian ruler, invited Jews to go back to their land beginning in 539 BC, many Jews were not interested in returning to Palestine. They had found a stable economy in their adopted land and they were prospering. They looked at the unstable economy of Palestine as uninviting.

These factors are rarely referred to in the Bible. The message supersedes all such detail, and the original readers knew all about it anyway. But for us to understand the message and the response of the people, we need to know these economic facts.

Culture influences thought patterns and language. The basic needs and desires of people are similar in all parts of the world and in many historical periods. But the thought patterns and language by which they express these needs have significant differences.

We can observe our own changes in thought patterns by comparing the *King James Version* with more modern translations. In both Greek and Hebrew, the kidneys were considered to be the center of emotions. Kidneys was translated "reins" in the King James. Psalm 16:7 reads "My reins [kidneys] also instruct me in the night seasons." Revelation 2:23 says, "I am he which searcheth the reins and hearts." Contemporary translations such as the *Revised Standard Version* and the *New International Version* usually use "heart" in such places, since in our culture we think of the heart as the symbolic center of emotion.

"Bowels" are often referred to as the seat of kindness and other feelings. In the *King James Version*, 1 John 3:17 reads, "But whoso hath this world's good, and seeth his brother have need, and shutteth up his bowels of compassion from him, how dwelleth the love of God in him?" Most modern translations use "heart" where the *KJV* uses "bowels."

In other parts of the world these ideas must be translated into appropriate local forms. In the Sudanic languages of northern Congo, for example, the liver is considered the center of a person's inward being. In this culture, Matthew 15:8 should be translated, "These people honor me with their lips, but their livers are far from me." The missionary of today needs to understand the cultural thought of the early readers of the Bible, the thought patterns of his own culture, and also those of the people to whom he ministers.

God's message came to people in a distinct cultural setting different from our own. We cannot really understand what it means in our own culture unless we first understand what it meant in the original culture.

Dealing with History and Culture

1. In a Bible atlas or dictionary, find out what you

can about the places that provide the geographical setting for the part of the Bible you are studying.

2. Determine what historical period is most likely for the passage. Remember that the historical *situation* is more important than the precise historical date.

3. Know as much as you can about the people involved in the section of the Bible you are studying.

4. Try to see how the history preceding the time of the original hearers or readers influenced their responses and attitudes.

5. Watch for customs, objects of material culture, and socio-religious relationships in the section you are studying.

6. Try to see how the message of the passage transcends its immediate surroundings.

7. Be sensitive to the similarities and differences between our culture and that of the original writer and his readers. This will help us make proper applications to our own lives.

Questions for Discussion

1. To consider historical cultural backgrounds, read through the book of Philemon. (It is only one chapter and will take you less than 15 minutes.) Consult a commentary on Philemon, or a Bible dictionary or encyclopedia. Look up the entries on *Philemon, Colossae, slavery.*

   a. What did you learn about the historical factors behind the book of Philemon?
   b. Do you think an understanding of slavery in the Roman Empire is important in understanding the book of Philemon?
   c. How does our historical situation differ from Philemon's? How is it alike? What

applications can we honestly draw from this book?

2. To compare the faith situation and the life situation, read through the entire book of Haggai. (Again you can do it in less than 15 minutes.)

 a. What is the "life situation"—the history and problems of the people during the time it was written? (You can get all of this from the book itself.)

 b. What do we have in common with the situation of the first readers?

 c. In what ways do we have differences? How will this influence our interpretation?

 d. What lesson can be seen from Haggai that is applicable to our lives?

Chapter 7

What Is This Passage Talking About?

Most of us have had at least one experience with someone incorrectly quoting what we said or wrote. The error may have been in changing or eliminating or adding one or two words so that it came out with a different meaning. Or it may have been that the correct quotation was taken out of its context so that its meaning was distorted. This is frustrating because we cannot deny that we actually said or wrote those words, but the meaning now given to them is not what we originally intended.

How frustrated the biblical writers probably would be if they could hear how the things they wrote are often used! Preachers and laymen alike are guilty of this misuse. Remarkably fine sermons have often been hung on a line or two of Scripture taken out of context. Regardless of how fine and uplifting the sermon may be, it is a kind of dishonesty to try to give authority to *our* ideas by implying that the Scriptures we are quoting uphold what we are saying.

Examine the Context of the Passage

The exact meaning of a passage of Scripture is normally controlled by what precedes and what follows a specific thought. What precedes and what follows form the *context* of the passage.

Biblical writers usually expressed themselves in series of related ideas, sometimes tied together loosely by a general theme, but basically supported by the ideas preceding and following the specific thought. To know what the Bible means by a specific passage, we need to know what the writer said before and after that passage.

To study in depth any section, we often need to read quickly through the whole book. Suppose we are studying Ephesians 3:4-6. We need to know the general purpose of the letter to the Ephesians. We cannot know this until we read the whole of Ephesians. By reading through the entire book, we can see the total purpose of the letter.

Make your own headings. As we read, it is wise to summarize in a few words the main point of each paragraph. If possible, write these words in the margin of your Bible. Although a summary prepared by a biblical scholar may be more correct professionally than yours, it will never stay with you as your own summary will. Besides, when you make your own headings, you must *think* about what you are reading.

If you went through the book of Ephesians, writing paragraph headings, you would find that most of the first chapter is a picture of God's glorious plan of salvation and a prayer that the readers would know and experience that glory.

Chapters 2 and 3 discuss the unity of all believers in Christ. Ephesians 2:1-10 tells what it means to be made alive in Christ. Ephesians 2:11-22 discusses the Gentiles' equal share with Jewish Christians in the blessings of the new life in Christ.

Chapter 3 deals with this remarkable oneness of Gentile and Jewish believers in Christ. The way Paul emphasizes this idea indicates how important it was to him, as a Jewish believer writing to Gentile Christians. Since there are so few Jewish Christians in our churches today, the subject does not seem so important to us. Other divisions polarize us far more than that one. But perhaps Paul's teachings about the Jewish-Gentile divisions of his day may throw light on how we can handle the divisions of our day.

Chapters 4 to 6 give practical instructions on how we as believers are to conduct ourselves in the light of our position in Christ.

Check what comes before the passage you are studying. After thinking about the overall context of Ephesians, look at the immediate context. Ephesians 3:4-6 is part of a section where Paul discusses the relationship of Jew and Gentile to God. Just preceding this (2:14-16), Paul develops the idea of the union of Jews and Gentiles in the church. God, through the reconciliation of Christ, makes the two—Jew and Gentile—into one person, the Christian. All Christians (Jews and Gentiles) are part of one body—the church. Through Christ, Jews and Gentiles may approach God in one Spirit (2:18). The Gentiles who were once "strangers and sojourners" are now fellow citizens with the saints—the Jewish saints—and are all now part of the "household of God" (2:19).

Knowing what is in chapter 2 is essential to understanding Ephesians 3:4-6: "When you read this you can perceive my insight into the mystery of Christ, which was not made known to the sons of men in other generations as it has now been revealed to his holy apostles and prophets by the Spirit; that is, how the Gentiles are fellow heirs, members of the same body, and partakers of the promise in Christ Jesus through the gospel."

Note Ephesians 3:6: "how the Gentiles are fellow heirs, members of the same body, and partakers of the promise in Christ Jesus through the gospel." If we did not know what came before this in chapter 2, we would ask, "Fellow heirs with whom? Members of the same body as who? Partakers with whom of the promise in Christ Jesus?" But the previous chapter has already told us that Paul is talking about the "mystery" of Jewish believers and Gentile believers being brought together in Christ.

Examine what follows the passage you are studying. Notice Ephesians 3:7-10: "Of this gospel I was made a minister according to the gift of God's grace which was given me by the working of his power. To me, though I am the very least of all the saints, this grace was given, to preach to the Gentiles the unsearchable riches of Christ, and to make all men see what is the plan of the mystery hidden for ages in God who created all things; that through the church the manifold wisdom of God might now be made known to the principalities and powers in the heavenly places."

Paul is here explaining that his main calling is to bring the good news to the Gentiles. To them he proclaimed what had previously been a secret (v. 9). This "mystery" or secret was the way God would bring all people, Jews and Gentiles, into a living relationship with Himself.

Study parallel writings in the Bible. Similar ideas or teachings are often found in several parts of the Bible. One passage often reinforces or throws additional light on another. These are called parallel passages. In a true parallel, a writer often gives a fuller version of an incident or parable or teaching than other writers. Consulting the various accounts gives a more complete picture. However, while parallels are extremely helpful, they can also be dangerous.

Sometimes what seems parallel is not. One passage may seem, on the surface, to be restating an idea found elsewhere in the Bible, but closer analysis may show this is not true. Only the context will tell whether ideas are really parallel.

For example, in Ephesians 3:3-6, the "mystery of Christ" is that the Jew and Gentile are made "one new person" by belief in Christ. But Paul uses the word "mystery" again in Colossians 1:25-27: "I became a minister according to the divine office which was given to me for you, to make the word of God fully known, the mystery hidden for ages and generations but now made manifest to his saints. To them God chose to make known how great among the Gentiles are the riches of the glory of this mystery, which is Christ in you, the hope of glory."

This sounds somewhat like the passage in Ephesians. But here Paul clearly defines the "mystery" as "Christ in you, the hope of glory." The two ideas are certainly related, but they are not identical. Ephesians 3:6 cannot be used to define the mystery in Colossians 1:27 or vice versa. The verses in Ephesians discuss and define *part* of the mystery about which Paul writes in Colossians—Christ in you, the hope of glory.

Examples of true parallel writings are often found in the Gospels. Four writers recorded the teachings and life of Christ. A parallel study of their accounts is important. In some places, Jesus' teachings are arranged chronologically; other times they are grouped by subject matter. No doubt Jesus often repeated His teachings in His travels throughout Galilee and Perea. Sometimes He expounded to His disciples at length about a subject that He had previously mentioned to the crowds who gathered to hear Him.

To understand Jesus' teachings on any subject, we must study all of the parallels, carefully considering them in their context.

If we are studying Jesus' teachings about peace and the use of force, we might turn to all of the passages that deal with a sword. In Matthew 10:34-36, Jesus says, "Do not suppose that I have come to bring peace to the earth. I did not come to bring peace, but a sword. For I have come to turn 'a man against his father, a daughter against her mother, a daughter-in-law against her mother-in-law—a man's enemies will be the members of his own household' " (*NIV*).

To whom did Jesus say these words and under what circumstances? The context shows that Jesus was warning His disciples of the troubles that would come to them as they went forth to proclaim the Kingdom of God.

We find similar teachings in Mark 13:13, "And you will be hated by all for my name's sake. But he who endures to the end will be saved."

When Jesus was being captured by the soldiers in the garden on the night before He was crucified, He talked about the sword again after one of His disciples had cut off the ear of one of the slaves of the high priest. Jesus said to him, "Put your sword back into its place; for all who take the sword will perish by the sword" (Matt. 26:52).

This incident appears in all four Gospels. Only Matthew includes the saying, "All who take the sword will perish by the sword." Only John reveals that the disciple who used the sword was Peter (John 18:10) and that the name of the slave was Malchus.

The account of Luke, on the other hand, says that before Jesus went to Gethsemane to pray, He said to His disciples, "Let him who has no sword sell his mantle and buy one" (Luke 22:36). When the disciples told Him they had two swords, Jesus said, "It is enough" (Luke 22:38).

Thus it is important in studying any subject to find all the passages in the Bible that deal with that subject and to examine the context in which each is used so that we do not misinterpret the meaning or read our own meaning into the words of the writer.

Words do not always have the same meaning. When studying any subject in the Bible it is easy to forget that words may have several possible meanings. We know this is true for our own language. Consider the word "rest." If a person in the middle of a hot day says he wants to rest, he probably means he wants to take a nap. If we say, "She was laid to rest in a quiet garden," we mean she was buried.

A similar thing occurs often in the Bible. Paul uses the word "flesh" several ways. In Romans 8:12,13, he says, "So then, brethren, we are debtors, not to the flesh, to live according to the flesh—for if you live according to the flesh you will die, but if by the Spirit you put to death the deeds of the body you will live." In this passage where Paul contrasts "flesh" with "Spirit," he is using flesh to mean "self-centeredness."

Paul uses "flesh" with a different meaning in Philippians 1:22-24. "If it is to be life in the flesh, that means fruitful labor for me. Yet which I shall choose I cannot tell. I am hard pressed between the two. My desire is to depart and be with Christ, for that is far better. But to remain in the flesh is more necessary on your account." In this passage, flesh obviously refers to the physical body that can die.

The context must determine the meaning of a biblical word, just as context determines meaning in our own speech. We must also be sure that the meaning we are giving is one that was normally used with that word in the original language among the original readers. For example, the word "head" did not normally connote "authority over" in the Greek language. We must be sure not to read our figurative meanings into those of other languages.[1]

Recognize Topical Groupings

Some sections of the Old and New Testaments actually give no context. Proverbs and Ecclesiastes are collections of sayings, proverbs, and epigrams for which no immediate context is given. However, the editor or collector of these sayings often grouped them together by topic.

This kind of grouping also occurs occasionally in the Gospels, especially in the sayings of Jesus. For example, in Luke 16:14-18 five topics are discussed in five verses.

verse	*topic*
14. The Pharisees, who were lovers of money, heard all this, and they scoffed at him.	The Pharisees ridiculed Jesus for His teachings about wealth.
15. But he said to them, "You are those who justify	Jesus declares God's knowledge of people's

yourselves before men, but God knows your hearts; for what is exalted among men is an abomination in the sight of God.

hearts.

16. "The law and the prophets were until John; since then the good news of the kingdom of God is preached, and everyone enters it violently.

The law and the prophets were until John, plus the proclamation and response to the Kingdom of God.

17. "But it is easier for heaven and earth to pass away, than for one dot of the law to become void.

The disappearance of heaven and earth are easier than to make invalid the smallest part of the law.

18. "Everyone who divorces his wife and marries another commits adultery, and he who marries a woman divorced from her husband commits adultery."

Divorce

What can we do in these situations? One step is to try to find genuine parallels in another book by the same author or in another book from the same general time period. For example, Luke 16:18 discusses divorce, but there is a fuller account with more context in Matthew 19:3-12.

Faithful examination of context will help us appreciate what was said to the first hearers or readers and how or if it should be carried over to our own times.

Questions for Discussion

Choose a short book that can be read through quickly; 2 John is a good example. Read it all the way through.

1. Read it through again and put in paragraph headings in the margin of your Bible. (You can change the paragraphing if you disagree with the places where your translator placed the paragraphs. Paragraphs were not a part of the original text.)

2. Choose one or two verses that seem meaningful to you and that you would like to study more. For example, you might choose verses 5 and 6.

3. Notice what ideas come *before* your chosen verses. How does that influence the meaning of your chosen verses?

4. Notice what comes *after* your chosen verses. Does the meaning you are giving the verses make good sense with what follows?

5. What else does this author say about the subject in this chapter? (If you are using a passage from a longer book, you would ask what else the author says about this subject in the rest of the book.) What does the author say in his other writings?

If you chose verses 5 and 6, use a concordance to see what else John says in his other writings about loving one another. For example, look at 1 John 4:7-21. Are his other writings on this subject consistent with the meaning you are giving to "love one another" in this passage? Do his other writings give additional light on the subject?

Note

1. For additional information on the Greek meaning of "head" see article "The 'Head' of the Epistles" in *Christianity Today*, Feb. 20, 1981, by Berkeley and Alvera Mickelsen.

Chapter 8

The Bible Is Rich in Figurative Language

When we speak of figurative language in the Bible, some Christians become worried. They think that seeing something as figurative means that it is imaginary or unreal. This is a misunderstanding.

In this book, the word *literal* refers to what a word or phrase means in its ordinary, customary usage. The word *figurative* refers to the meaning of a word or expression when it is compared to something else. Making such a comparison is called an analogy. When Jesus said, "I am the bread of life" (John 6:35), He used figurative language—an analogy. He meant that He is to people spiritually what bread is to people physically—the sustainer of life. The figurative meaning of bread here has even greater significance and is even more real than the literal or ordinary meaning.

We use these kinds of comparisons and imagery constantly when we explain things to children. A child asks, "What is a cloud like inside? Is it like cotton?"

And a parent answers, "No, a cloud is not like cotton. It is more like thick fog." Something known to the child by experience—thick fog—is used to explain something not known—the feeling of a cloud.

We all use short figures of speech freely in our own language. When we say, "He is an eager beaver," or "She is an iceberg," the meaning is clear to the listener. It does *not* mean that the man has a flat tail like a beaver or that the woman is huge like an iceberg. It refers instead to *one* important characteristic that the person shares in common with whatever is being compared. And we recognize immediately what that relevant point of comparison is.

In biblical figures of speech, that relevant point of comparison was no doubt obvious to the original listener or reader. We must be sure we know what that point of comparison is and *not push the figure of speech beyond that point.*

Figures of Speech Are Common in the Bible

Jesus, the master teacher, constantly taught new truths by using what was familiar to His listeners. So skillful was Jesus in His use of figurative language that His listeners often were hardly aware that He had used a figure, but His message came home immediately and sharply.

Jesus chose His figurative language from areas of life familiar to His listeners. He talked of foxes, sheep, birds, the mustard seed, the leafing of trees, fruit-growing, the signs of the weather.

He chose imagery from wedding customs, father-son relationships, qualities of children, parts of houses (door, key), household tasks such as mending, sweeping, sewing, cooking.

For Jesus, imagery and analogy was the language of life. Old Testament prophets also used figurative language profusely. It is important to recognize such language.

Jesus taught through similes—comparisons explicitly stated with words such as "like" or "as." When Jesus sent out the seventy disciples in Luke 10:1-3, He told them exactly what to expect. "Behold, I send you out *as* lambs in the midst of wolves" (v. 3, italics added). Jesus recognized growing animosity toward Himself. He had fierce enemies (wolves) and the disciples (lambs) had no experience in such conflict. The word which shows that this is a simile is "as."

In Matthew 23:37, Jesus looked over Jerusalem and said, "How often would I have gathered your children together *as* a hen gathers her brood under her wings, and you would not!" (italics added). The points of comparison are the concern and care the hen gives its chicks, and the love and care Jesus wanted to give His own people.

Jesus used another simile to describe His second coming. Matthew 24:26,27 reads, "So, if they say to you, 'Lo, he is in the wilderness,' do not go out; if they say, 'Lo, he is in the inner rooms,' do not believe it. For *as* the lightning comes from the east and shines as far as the west, so will be the coming of the Son of man."

The comparison (indicated by "as") is that the coming of Christ will be as visible as the lightning that can be seen from east to west. Jesus apparently used this simile to correct any erroneous ideas of a secret coming of Christ in some desert place or inner room.

Similes are common in both Old and New Testaments. The book of Revelation is profuse with them. Revelation has so many, in fact, that the reader needs to think about each one with questions like these: Why did John feel he should use a simile in this place? How does the simile help us to understand the idea being presented? Even with the simile, what in this passage is still unknown to the reader or is understood in only a general way?

While thankful for the illumination that similes bring, we must not try to make them say more than they are meant to convey. Similes are like wild flowers: if we cultivate them too vigorously, they lose their beauty.

Metaphors are common in the Bible. A metaphor is a figure of speech in which the writer describes one thing in terms of something else.

In Luke 12:32, Jesus said, "Fear not, *little flock*, for it is your Father's good pleasure to give you the kingdom" (italics added).

This metaphor of describing believers as a flock of sheep is continued in John 10:16. "And I have other sheep, that are not of this fold; I must bring them also, and they will heed my voice. So there shall be one flock, one shepherd." Through this metaphor, Jesus taught His concept of the church.

With another metaphor, Jesus taught that spiritual ties are stronger and more important than physical ties. "My mother and my brothers are those who hear the word of God and do it" (Luke 8:21).

Many metaphors in the Old the New Testaments describe God's power in terms of body parts and physical movements. These are technically known as *anthropomorphisms*. "Behold, the *Lord's hand* is not shortened that it cannot save, or *his ear* dull, that it cannot hear" (Isa. 59:1, italics added). Another anthropomorphism, "the arm of the Lord" appears many times in the Old Testament. We know that God does not have a physical arm, nor an ear, nor a hand. Yet this metaphorical language gives a more vivid picture of the power of God than would a theological treatise on omnipotence.

Another kind of metaphor, known as *anthropopathism*, is used to ascribe to God human emotions, feelings, and responses. God's *grief* is mentioned in Genesis 6:6 and in Ephesians 4:30. God's *wrath* is referred to in John 3:36, Revelation 14:10; 15:1,7, and in other places. His *anger* plays a prominent role in Job 9:13, Jonah 3:9, and Mark 3:5.

Is this metaphorical language? Does God not actually experience grief, wrath, and anger? The answer is yes, but not really in the same sense as people. Human emotion is highly complex. Grief often involves self-pity; anger tends to be laced with a desire for revenge. Yet an accurate picture of God's grief and God's anger must exclude such sinful responses. God's response is not tainted by corrupt elements.

When we deal with this kind of metaphorical language in the Bible, we must remove the self-centeredness that is so often a part of these emotions. When we say, "God loves," "God is angry," or "God is pleased," we must not mix into these ideas the sinful elements that often are a part of human love or anger or pleasure. God is *not* an enlarged human being.

Words of association often appear in the Bible. These are common in our own language. In the United States, "White House" has become a synonym for the president. "The White House decided to release the speech today," really refers to the president or those with his delegated authority. Substitutions like this are natural to our thinking and they were natural to the thinking of the writers of Scripture. Sometimes, however, the association is not as clear to us as it was to the original readers or hearers. For example, Ephraim (one of the ten tribes of the Northern kingdom) is often used as a synonym for the entire Northern kingdom of Israel, and Judah became the name for the Southern kingdom which actually included the tribes of Judah, Simeon, and part of Benjamin.

Paul used association with the terms "circumcision" and "uncircumcision." Romans 3:30 says, "He [God] will justify the circumcised on the ground of their faith and the uncircumcised through their faith." The context shows that "circumcised" stands for Jews and "uncircumcised" stands for Gentiles.

In other figures of speech a whole is used for a part or a part for a whole. An individual may be used for a class of people or a class for an individual. In Romans 1:16, Paul wrote, "For I am not ashamed of the gospel: it is the power of God for salvation to every one who has faith, to the Jew first and also to the Greek." "The Jew" and "the Greek" obviously means the *Jews* and the *Greeks*.

Judges 12:7, literally translated, says, "And Jephthah judged Israel for six years. Then Jephthah, the Gileadite, died, and he was buried in the *cities* of Gilead." Jephthah obviously could not be buried in more than *one* city. Why does the text read *cities*? Although Jephthah had served the interests of all the tribes of Israel, his own tribe *as a group* claimed his burial place. Most translators of this passage have added the words *one of* in italics before "the cities" to indicate an addition to the original text. But this figure of speech indicating *a group as one* underlines the strength of Israel's tribal ties.

One picturesque figure of speech of this type

appears in Micah 4:3 and Isaiah 2:4. "And they shall beat their swords into plowshares, and their spears into pruning hooks." The abandonment of two weapons—swords and spears—stands for total disarmament.

The picture is reversed in Joel 3:10, which says, "Beat your plowshares into swords, and your pruning hooks into spears." This is far more dramatic than to say, "Arm yourselves for war; organize the people for military conflict."

Poetic figures of personification. In personification, personal qualities are ascribed to an object or an idea. Jesus often used this figure of speech. In Matthew 6:34, He said, "Therefore do not be anxious about tomorrow, for tomorrow will be anxious for itself." Anxiety is a quality of people, not of days or tomorrows, but Jesus chose this picturesque way of describing the folly of torturing ourselves by unnecessary worry about the future.

The Psalms are full of vivid personifications. In Psalm 114, the writer celebrates God's delivery of the Jews from Egypt. He writes (in poetry):

"The sea looked and fled,
Jordan turned back.
The mountains skipped like rams,
The hills like lambs.

. . . .

Tremble, O earth, at the presence of the Lord,
at the presence of the God of Jacob" (vv. 3,4,7).

Euphemisms in the Bible. Euphemism is a kind of understatement often used in the Bible. It is the substitution of a more indirect or delicate term for a blunt one that may be offensive or distasteful. We use a euphemism when we say "he passed away" rather than "he died."

When the Old Testament discusses sex it often uses euphemistic language. Leviticus 18:6, translated literally, reads, "Every man of you shall not come near unto flesh of his flesh to uncover nakedness." Translators usually clarify the first phrase "flesh of his flesh" by making it "near of kin" or "blood relatives." But the phrase "to uncover nakedness" is an Old Testament euphemism for sexual intercourse or marriage contract. The passage in Leviticus is a warning against incest.

Perhaps the right kind of euphemisms would be worth considering for our day. The Old Testament language is direct enough so that the first readers, the Hebrew people, knew exactly what was being discussed. At the same time there is no morbid preoccupation with details. The Old Testament is neither prudish nor prurient in dealing with sex. Euphemism helped achieve this.

Hyperbole must be recognized and understood in the Bible. Hyperbole means conscious exaggeration and is common in our own speech. We say laughingly, "I could kill you for that remark," when we really mean we are mildly annoyed. If a person says, "After a day like today, I'm dead," we know he or she means, "I'm tired."

Hyperbole abounds in every language, including the languages of the Bible. Jesus used it freely. He said: "If your right eye causes you to sin, pluck it out and throw it away; it is better that you lose one of your members than that your whole body be thrown into hell. And if your right hand causes you to sin, cut it off and throw it away" (Matt. 5:29,30).

Rational people do not chop off their hands or

pluck out their eyes. Jesus' hyperbole says that it is more important for a person to be whole and well spiritually than that he or she be whole and well physically. Spiritual welfare takes precedence over physical welfare.

Unfortunately, not every instance of hyperbole is so easy to recognize. Immediately after the passage mentioned above, Jesus discusses divorce, saying, "Every one who divorces his wife, except on the ground of unchastity, makes her an adulteress; and whoever marries a divorced woman commits adultery." Is this hyperbole? The answer is not easy and becomes a matter of interpretation and judgment. Whether we take it literally or as hyperbole, the message is still clear: marriage is sacred and God intends it to be permanent.

This passage should be considered with Matthew 5:27,28, which also deals with adultery. Here Jesus said, "You have heard that it was said, 'You shall not commit adultery.' But I say to you that everyone who looks [as a constant or customary activity] at a woman lustfully has already committed adultery with her in his heart." Is this hyperbole? Does Jesus actually mean that lustful looks are the equivalent of adultery in the eyes of God?

This example is given not to confuse the reader but to show how complex are the problems revolving around the interpretation of such simple figures of speech as the hyperboles used by Jesus.

Irony appears in the Bible. In irony, the writer or speaker means the exact opposite of what the words say. If two friends meet on a blistering hot day and one says to the other, "I'm freezing, Joe; how are you doing?" we recognize this as irony.

To the query, "How was the exam?" a student may

reply, "You know Professor Smith. He always gives exams that are a snap." Yet the tone of voice indicates that he means exactly the opposite—that Professor Smith always gives difficult exams and this one was no exception.

Irony is a vivid tool in writing, but since we cannot hear the tone of voice of the speaker, careful study of the context is essential if we are to recognize the irony.

Jesus used irony effectively, but because we cannot hear the tone of voice in which He spoke, we sometimes fail to recognize it.

In Matthew 23, Jesus pronounced a long list of woes against the Pharisees, outlining in detail their previous sins and heaping scorn on their self-righteous claims that if they had been living in the days of their fathers, they would not have murdered the prophets as their ancestors did.

Then Jesus said, "Fill up, then, the measure of your fathers" (Matt. 23:32). This is irony. The Pharisees were bent on destroying Jesus. No miracles that Jesus did, none of His teachings changed their attitudes. Jesus is giving them up to their self-chosen destiny. He is saying in essence, "Just keep right on with your sinning. Soon you can complete all the sins your fathers missed." Jesus was not baiting them or encouraging them to sin further by killing Him, but He was employing irony.

Paul used irony in 1 Corinthians 4:8. He had been discussing the partisan spirit in Corinth where groups were aligning themselves as being for Paul or Apollos or Cephas. Their boasting about being in one group or another showed that they felt like proud possessors rather than receivers. So Paul adds a note of irony: "Already you are filled! Already you have become rich! Without us you have become kings!" Paul used irony to strike out against their pride. The Corinthian Christians thought they were so rich in spiritual teaching that they could argue over which teacher was best. Paul adds, "Would that you did reign, so that we might share the rule with you!" He says that if this were only true then he and the other apostles would be free from their sufferings and oppression. Paul used irony to show the gulf between the imaginary and the real.

The figures of speech in the Bible enrich both its meaning and its literary value. But to gain full benefit from it, the reader needs to recognize what he is reading and interpret it accordingly.

Questions for Discussion

Read Isaiah 1:1-31. This chapter is full of figures of speech. There are similes, metaphors, personifications, anthropomorphisms and anthropopathisms.

1. Personifications (something non-human given human qualities)
   a. What is personified in verse 2? What does the personification add in meaning?
   b. What is personified in verses 5 and 6? What does it add to the meaning and vividness?
2. Similes and metaphors (comparisons)
   a. What is compared in verse 8? Note how some of the meaning of the comparison is lost because of changes in culture from that time to this. If the prophet were writing for readers in our day, what might he say instead of "like a booth in a vineyard; like a lodge in a cucumber field, like a beseiged city"? (Look up "booth" in a Bible dictionary to get the original meaning.)

    b. What is compared in verse 18? Note that "wool" to us is not automatically white. What might the prophet have said if he were writing in our day?

    c. What is compared in verse 30? What is the meaning in this figure of speech? Note that the comparison is built on verse 29 where "oaks" and "gardens" have a specific connection with idolatry (see Isa. 57:5 and 65:3). Look up "groves" in a Bible dictionary.

3. Anthropomorphisms and anthropopathisms (expressions that give God human qualities).

    a. What bodily parts does verse 15 attribute to God? What message does this give you about God?

    b. What human emotions are attributed to God in verses 10 to 14 and 24 to 26? Are these emotions in God different from similar emotions that you feel?

4. Hyperbole (conscious exaggeration). Read Luke 14:25-33.

    a. Are there examples of hyperbole in this passage?

    b. What is the message imbedded in the hyperbole? How do you know that it is hyperbole? If these verses were read with a literal meaning rather than as a hyperbole, do they contradict other teachings of the New Testament?

Chapter 9

Parables and Allegories

A parable is a short, fictional story that teaches a lesson by comparison. Parables usually focus on only one point of comparison.

An allegory is a story or teaching that is meant to convey a figurative meaning. It often involves several comparisons in which factors in the story or teaching stand for something specific.

Jesus used parables often; He used only a few allegories. Some of the differences can be seen by comparing the two:

In a parable	*In an allegory*
1. Words are used *literally*.	1. Words are used *figuratively*.
2. There is *one* chief point of comparison.	2. There are *several* points of comparison.
3. Imagery is kept *distinct* from the thing it signifies.	3. Imagery is *identified* with the things signified.

4. The meaning is explained by telling *what* the imagery stands for in light of the main point of the story.

4. The meaning is explained by showing *why* the imagery is identified with reality and what specific truths are taught.

5. The story is *true to the facts and experiences of life.*

5. The story *blends factual experience with non-factual experience* to enable the narrative to teach specific truths.

It is important to distinguish between *an allegory* and *allegorizing*. In allegorizing, a simple historical narrative or parable is made to teach something entirely different from that intended by the original writer. In allegorizing, the interpreter ignores what the original writer meant and looks instead for hidden meanings. By this method, the parables of Jesus and many of the stories of the Old and New Testaments have been much abused.

Allegorizing was common in the church from the time of Origen (AD 200) until the time of Luther (1500). Vestiges of this method still appear in some writing and preaching of our day.

Origen interpreted the story of the triumphal entry of Christ this way: The ass represents the letter of the Old Testament; the colt or foal of the ass speaks of the New Testament; the two apostles who obtained the animals and brought them to Jesus are the moral and spiritual senses.

One preacher in the fifth century allegorized on Herod's slaughter of the infants in Bethlehem this way: The fact that only children two years old and under were murdered while those age three presumably escaped is meant to teach us that those who believe in the Trinity will be saved whereas others will undoubtedly perish.

Such allegorizing tells the listener or reader what the *interpreter* is thinking but ignores the meaning of the biblical writer.

There is only one clear example of allegorizing in the New Testament—Galatians 4:21-31. In this passage Paul clearly tells us he is allegorizing when he says that Hagar and Sarah represent the two covenants: Hagar represents the Old Covenant (Judaism) and Mount Sinai; Sarah represents the New Covenant, the New Jerusalem.

The parables and allegories in the Bible are very different from the allegorizing of an historical narrative or a parable. Parables were not intended to be allegorized.

Parables of Jesus Focused on the Reign of God

Jesus' parables, like the rest of His teachings, usually focused on the *reign of God*. His teachings about the kingdom of God were really the center of His message. The Greek word *basileia*, meaning the royal reign or kingdom of God, appears more than a hundred times in the Gospels. Each of Jesus' parables usually illustrated some aspect of the reign of God.

In the parables of the tares (weeds) and the wheat (Matt. 13:24-30) Jesus showed that the reign of God is here now but is not absolute. The weeds are not uprooted now because the process might damage the wheat. "Let both grow together until the harvest" (Matt. 13:30) when the weeds will be burned and the wheat stored in the barn.

After explaining the parable to His disciples at a later time, Jesus described the consummation of history when the reign of God will be total: "The Son of man will send his angels, and they will gather out of his kingdom all causes of sin and all evildoers, and throw them into the furnace of fire; there men will weep and gnash their teeth. Then the righteous will shine like the sun in the kingdom of their Father (Matt. 13:41-43). This is all in the *future* tense, when the reign of God is complete.

Jesus underscored the *present* aspect of the reign of God in His parable about plundering a strong man's house by first binding the strong man. The Pharisees had accused Jesus of working His miracles by the power of Beelzebub, the prince of demons (Matt. 12:24; Mark 3:22). Jesus answered them with a series of short parables about a divided kingdom, a divided city, and a divided house that cannot stand (Matt. 12:25-29).

The parable of the strong man's house being plundered focused on Jesus' miracles as proof of His power to bind Satan. "If it is by the Spirit of God that I cast out demons, then the kingdom of God has come upon you" (Matt. 12:28). The miracles of Jesus were samples of Christ's power and what the reign of God will be like when it comes in its fullness.

In the two parables about the lost sheep and the lost coin in Luke 15:1-10, God's grace is shown when the shepherd and the woman take initiative to find what was lost. God rejoices over the response to His grace. In the parable of the lost sheep, God is represented by the shepherd. In the other, God is represented by the woman who lost the coin.

Two parables apply to great crises in the reign of

God. The first parable is that of the wicked tenants of the vineyard who killed the owner's son (Matt. 21:33-46; Mark 12:1-12; Luke 20:9-19). At the end of the parable, Jesus asked His listeners what the owner should do: the owner would destroy those tenants and give the vineyard to others. Matthew 21:43 records Jesus' application. "Therefore I tell you, the kingdom of God will be taken away from you and given to a nation producing the fruits of it."

The accounts in all three Gospels say that the Jewish leaders recognized that the parable was about them. Their anger was so great that they wanted to arrest Jesus immediately but were afraid of the crowd. This parable of crisis refers to Jesus' earthly life and death.

Another parable refers to a crisis yet to come in the reign of God—the return of Christ to complete His messianic work. This is the parable of the ten bridesmaids (or virgins)—five foolish and five wise (Matt. 25:1-13). The wise virgins were prepared at all times for the coming of the bridegroom; the foolish ones ran out of oil for their lamps. Jesus concluded with, "Watch therefore, for you know neither the day nor the hour" (Matt. 25:13).

When reading the parables, we must understand the main point of the story and note whether it deals with some aspect of the kingdom of God.

At the close of some of the parables, there is a terse teaching that sums up the lesson. Sometimes the same conclusion is attached to several parables. Jesus apparently used story after story to drive home certain important teachings.

The idea "The last will be first and the first last" (or some variation of it) appears several times. It appears with the parable about the workers who were hired at different times of day (Matt. 20:1-16); it appears following Jesus' interview with the rich young ruler (Matt. 19:16-30), and also with His teaching in Luke 13:22-30.

Allegories Are in Both Testaments

Allegories appear both in the Old and New Testaments, and their explanations often accompany them. In Proverbs 5:15-19, marital fidelity is extolled by urging that a man drink from his own cistern and no one else's. The explanation follows in verses 20 to 23 where the commandment is repeated in plain nonallegorical language.

A brilliant allegory appears in Ecclesiastes 12:3-7, where old age is depicted as a household that ceases to function.

In the New Testament there are several important allegories. One is of the vine and branches (John 15:1-10) and another is Paul's allegory of the building (1 Cor. 3:10-15). The Christian's armor is described in terms of weapons in Ephesians 6:10-17, and Christ is seen as the Good Shepherd in John 10:1-16.

Perhaps the most famous allegory is that of the Last Supper, which also included dramatization (Matt. 26:26-29; Mark 14:22-25; Luke 22:14-23). Jesus took bread and broke it, saying, "Take, eat; this is my body." Then He took the cup and said, "Drink of it, all of you; for this is my blood of the covenant, which is poured out for many for the forgiveness of sins" (Matt. 26:26-28).

That allegory has two parts and Jesus named them clearly—the bread, which is His body, and the wine, which is His blood, poured out for many for the forgiveness of sins. The fact that this is allegory does not make its truth less real.

The story of the vine and the branches (John 15:1-10) shows how Christ used allegory to teach something important. Jesus made three main comparisons.

The first stresses the importance of the vine (Christ) and its relationship to the branches (believers). "Apart from me, you [plural] can do nothing" (John 15:5).

The second comparison emphasizes the action of the vinedresser, the Father (John 15:1). The Father is concerned about fruit-bearing. He eliminates fruitless branches to bring to maximum production the branches attached to the vine.

The last major comparison is that of branches to believers (John 15:5). This illustrates one of the frequent characteristics of allegory—the blending of factual experience with non-factual experience so that the narrative can teach specific truths.

In the allegory of the vine and the branches, the branches "abide" in the vine. Actually, a real branch cannot choose to "abide" in the vine. It cannot truly choose to do anything. Yet in the allegory the disciples are commanded to "abide in me" as an obvious act of the will. Verse 6 reads, "If a man does not abide in me, he is cast forth as a branch and withers; and the branches are gathered, thrown into the fire and burned."

Obviously Jesus was not thinking of the inanimate connection of a branch to a vine. He was thinking of an active, vital relationship, for verse 7 reads, "If you abide in me, and my words abide in you, ask whatever you will, and it shall be done for you." Jesus was saying that answers to prayer demand this active relationship. The allegory dynamically portrays why the believer must maintain a fresh, vital relationship with Christ.

In the familiar allegory of the Good Shepherd in John 10:1-16, Jesus said that He represented the door of the sheepfold, and that He also represented the good shepherd. The sheep were those for whom Christ laid down His life. The flock represented the union of all believers regardless of their cultural or national heritage (John 10:7-16).

Difficulties with allegories arise when the interpreter goes beyond the explanation given in the Bible and insists that *every* point has to convey some specific comparison. For example, do we identify the hireling who fled (John 10:12) with the religious leaders of the day, or was it simply a part of the story inserted to bring out the true concern of the shepherd? It is not necessary to compare every point.

In dealing with both parables and allegories, it is important to try to see what Jesus or the writer was saying. In parables, we must understand the focus—the main point of the parable. In allegories, we should be satisfied with the interpretation given in the Bible and not go beyond that.

Questions for Discussion

1. Read the parable of the talents in Matthew 25:14-30.

    a. What do you think is the *main* point of the parable?

    b. How is the main point related to the reign of God—present or future?

    c. Do you think the generalized saying in Matt. 25:29,30 refers to the main point of the parable?

    d. What application do you think the parable

has to our own day? (Be sure to concentrate on the main point of the parable. Don't allegorize by trying to make every character stand for some specific thing or person.)

2. Study the allegory in Ecclesiastes 12:1-8.
   a. What basic comparison is used?
   b. In each of the following comparisons, what does old age mean?

      Sun, light and stars darkened
      Keepers of the house tremble
      Grinders cease because they are few
      Those who look through the windows are dimmed
      Doors on the street are shut
      Sound of the grinding is low
      Rises at the voice of a bird
      Afraid of what is high
      Afraid of terrors on the way
      Grasshopper drags itself along
      Desire fails
      Silver cord is snapped
         Golden bowl is broken
         Pitcher is broken at the fountain
         Wheel is broken at the cistern
   c. What is the main point of the allegory? (See Ecc. 12:1.)

Chapter 10

What Were the Prophets Saying?

To understand prophecy, we must first ask: What is a prophet? What is prophecy?

Prophets are spokesmen for God who declare God's message (prophecy) to their people.

At first glance, prophets seem to play a more important role in the Old Testament than in the New. Old Testament prophets superbly proclaimed the message of God both in warning and in promise. The prophets included both men and women—Deborah, Miriam, and Huldah are among the Old Testament prophets.

Prophets used drama, song, parable, story, and exhortation. They were used by God to examine, prove, and test the people (see Jer. 6:27). They proclaimed inevitable judgment as well as judgment that could be avoided if the people changed their ways. They acted both as watchmen and as intercessors.

Prophets in the New Testament had much in common with the Old Testament prophets, although there were some differences. Peter viewed the gift of prophecy as coming upon both men and women, old and young, and on all economic classes (slave and free) in fulfillment of the prophecy of Joel (Acts 2:16-18; Joel 2:28-32). Paul encouraged the Christians to strive for prophecy. In the New Testament, prophecy is a *gift* that all Christians may strive for and an *office* that God called only some Christians to hold.

The Purpose of Prophecy

Contrary to popular opinion, biblical prophecy was not primarily concerned with foretelling the future. In declaring God's will to the people, the prophet in his message might deal with the past, the present or the future. The prophet always had one basic aim in mind—to help people know God and His will for them.

Prophecy, according to 1 Corinthians 14, involves upbuilding, encouragement, consolation (14:3), edification (14:4), conviction and conversion (14:24,25) and instruction (14:31). These aspects of prophecy are sometimes called "forthtelling."

Prophecy (especially the future aspects or "foretelling") had a broad purpose. The prophets carried a message *from* God to their communities *about* their own communities and the nations surrounding them. The prophets usually were deeply involved in the life of their communities. They did not speak as outsiders but as those intimately identified with the people to whom they spoke.

In the Old Testament, the community was usually Israel, the people of God in the covenant nation. In the New Testament, the community was the church, the people of God of the New Covenant.

Unfortunately, many persons today think of prophecy only in terms of foretelling future events.

"Prophetic experts" today sometimes ignore those parts of prophecy that deal with the past or present lives of the first hearers or readers of the passage, and concentrate instead on the future. And the more future the better! Some try to read a prophecy about jet airplanes into certain Old Testament passages to show how futuristic the thinking of the prophet was. This kind of interpretation piles confusion on confusion regarding the nature of the prophet's message.

Every item of predictive prophecy was given to a particular historical people to awaken and call them to righteousness by revealing in part what God would do in the future. Any disclosure about the future was given to *influence their present action*. Probably the only way a description of a jet airplane could have influenced the people's action during Old Testament times would have been to increase their age-long desire to fly as a bird or to make them more fearful of the military use of such a machine.

Predictive prophecy was never given to satisfy our curiosity about the future. The future aspect of prophecy was intended to instruct, reprove, encourage and call people to repentance. The New Testament often uses phrases such as "behold the days are coming when," and "in those days." Such passages show that God is at work, advancing His program according to His schedule. Throughout the Bible runs the theme that there will be many crises followed by a mighty climax when the age to come will break through in its totality. God will then reign supreme. His will is to be done on earth as in heaven.

Two Erroneous Views of Predictive Prophecy

In recent years, two erroneous views have risen that have gained a surprising number of adherents.

One erroneous view is that *predictive prophecy is a vivid way of writing history*. This view is held by many who assume that real prediction is impossible in a universe governed wholly by cause and effect. Those who hold this view insist that God never revealed objective truths about Himself; He simply revealed Himself in events that would mean nothing to a person lacking faith.

However, much biblical material appears to the average prudent person to be predictive prophecy. The purveyors of this theory say that most of the apparently predictive materials were really written *after* the events they predict. The prophetic style was used to liven up the narrative of history and make it more interesting. If this theory did not seem to fit certain prophetic messages, those messages are generalized and called a brilliant insight by a prophet whose mind refused to be shut up within the confines of Hebrew daily life. This is part of the reason some critics date some books of the Old Testament very late. They *had* to be written after the events they describe to support the theory of the scholar.

But there are serious weaknesses in this view. Ordinary historical material in the Bible is not enigmatic like prophecy. Biblical history deals with many details and follows a basic chronological pattern. In contrast, the predictive prophetic narratives do not give subordinate details in any consistent train of thought or in any developed time sequences. Any person who could write history in the form of Hebrew prophecy would have to forget half of what he or she knew in order to give the appearance of being a prophet, and the artificiality of such a tactic could not be hidden.

The second erroneous view is at the opposite

extreme. The idea that *predictive prophecy is history written in advance* is just as erroneous as the idea that it is history written after the event. And it is wrong for somewhat the same reasons. Predictive prophecy is enigmatic. It never gives enough details to substitute for a historical summary.

Assume for a moment that the circle below contains the fewest possible elements or facts necessary to picture a definite historical event. Each "x" represents one of these needed elements.

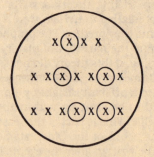

The x's that are circled represent the facts in a historical event that were revealed in advance to and by the prophet. These alone obviously leave many crucial elements missing. But if prophecy were simply history written beforehand, all of the x's would be circles and the enigmatic character of predictive prophecy would disappear.

For example, Matthew 4:14 says that the prophet Isaiah foretold Jesus' Galilean ministry. Isaiah 9:1,2 reads: "In the former time he brought into contempt the land of Zebulun and the land of Naphtali, but in the latter time he will make glorious the way of the sea, the land beyond the Jordan, Galilee of the nations.

"The people who walked in darkness
have seen a great light;
those who dwelt in a land of deep darkness,
on them has light shined."

"The way of the sea" meant the ancient caravan route that ran from Damascus to the Mediterranean. "Beyond the Jordan" referred to the land on the east side of the Jordan and the Sea of Galilee. "Galilee of the nations" was the northern borders of upper and lower Galilee and was singled out as that part of the land which had been especially dishonored but at a later time would be honored. A people whose course of action was in darkness (the Gentiles) would see a great light.

These words were fulfilled during the ministry of Jesus. Then why was it not history written beforehand? Because the *historical* record of the New Testament must be read to see just where Jesus carried on His ministry in Galilee and in what sense "the people who walked in darkness saw a great light."

The Gospels show that the Galilean ministry of Jesus was largely limited to His own Jewish people. He was the light that shone brightly in the darkness *of His own people.*

During Jesus' earthly ministry He had contact with only a few Gentiles. However, through the ministry of the early church, many Gentiles did come to see the Great Light that illumined their darkness.

Prophecy cannot be history written beforehand because God does not disclose enough of the major and minor elements essential for even an incomplete *historical* account. What God makes known as well as what He withholds are part of the total plan of redemption. As history moves on, the full-orbed picture emerges. Earlier intimations of what is to come remind us that all of history is in God's sovereign control.

How False Prophets Received Their Messages

Did the prophets actually receive their messages from God? Could they not pretend or be deceived into thinking they had received a divine message in order to have a position of prominence among the people? Perhaps the prophet was self-deluded, thinking he or she was a messenger of God, when in reality the message came from hallucinations or mental illness. Is this possible?

Prophets of that kind are mentioned in the Scriptures. Jeremiah 14:14 says, "And the Lord said to me: 'The prophets are prophesying lies in my name; I did not send them, nor did I command them or speak to them. They are prophesying to you a lying vision, worthless divination, and the deceit of their own minds.' "

Such prophets created their own material without any genuine relationship with God. In one sense, true prophets also created their own material, for each one's individual style is stamped on his or her message, but they did not originate their messages. They stood in a vital relationship to God and it was God who spoke as well as the prophets.

How True Prophets Received Their Messages

Occasionally God spoke to His prophets in dreams or night visions. Paul saw in a dream the man of Macedonia saying, "Come over to Macedonia and help us" (Acts 16:9). The dreams or visions seem to be the ordinary dreams of the night, with power to retain what was dreamed. (It does not follow, of course, that *our* dreams are revelations of God!)

Prophets often received their messages when they were in an ecstatic state. This was not self-induced excitement in which the prophet jumped around in an irrational manner. Rather, the prophet's mental and spiritual faculties rose to a new level of performance.

The prophet Habakkuk tells of stationing himself on a tower to *see* what God would say to him. He was alert and prepared for God to reveal something to him. Most such ecstatic experiences occurred in the daytime—only a few at night. Perhaps the best modern analogy would be closed-circuit television. The prophet is sometimes said to "see" the word or message of the Lord (Isa. 2:1; Micah 1:1). At other times, the prophets saw visions, utterances, oracles, or revelations (Isa. 1:1; Ezek. 1:1; 13:16). The visions from God were *content-centered*.

Jeremiah 14:14 shows what the Lord *did not do* for false prophets. The false prophets "are prophesying lies in my name; I did not send them, nor did I command them or speak to them. They are prophesying to you a lying vision, worthless divination, and the deceit of their own minds."

By reversing this we can see what the Lord *did do* for true prophets: God sent them, commanded them, spoke to them. They prophesied visions of truth.

God sometimes revealed His message to His prophets through direct communication without dreams or ecstatic visions. This kind of direct communication occurred many times in the Old Testament. One such example occurred when King Hezekiah was very ill. Second Kings 20:1-6 tells that Isaiah came to him with a message from God that he was going to die. Hearing Isaiah's message, Hezekiah prayed fervently, asking the Lord to remember that he was a king who had faithfully served God. Isaiah left Hezekiah after delivering the message of impending death. On his way out of the palace, Isaiah met God. "And before Isaiah had gone out of the middle court, the word of the Lord came to him" (2 Kings 20:4). Isaiah was told to go back and tell Hezekiah that God would heal him and give him fifteen additional years, and that Jerusalem would be delivered from the oppression of the king of Assyria.

Isaiah did not have a vision or a dream. While awake, fully alert and active, he received a direct message from God.

Prophets Were Personally Involved in Events

Prophets were often deeply involved in specific historical events of their day. In the midst of this personal involvement the prophet may have received an authoritative message from God.

In a time of severe crisis King Jehoiakim burned up the scroll produced at the command of God by Jeremiah and his secretary, Baruch (Jer. 36:1-32). The king ordered Jeremiah and Baruch imprisoned, but they hid. Then the word of the Lord came to Jeremiah again. He was to prepare another scroll like the one the king burned. He reproduced the first book and added some to it. Included in the second version was the prophecy that Jehoiakim would be slain and not even have the honor of being buried.

Jeremiah became unwillingly involved in another prophecy at the end of his life. After many of the leaders of Judah were deported to Babylon, the king of Babylon appointed Gedaliah to govern those who were left in Palestine. Gedaliah was murdered and the remaining men feared reprisals. They asked Jeremiah if they should stay or try to escape to Egypt.

They promised to obey whatever the Lord told them. Jeremiah had to wait ten days before he received the answer from the Lord: if they would stay in Palestine, God would establish them. If they went to Egypt, they would be blotted out. Even while Jeremiah was delivering the message, he sensed that his hearers had already made up their minds. They all fled to Egypt despite the prophecy, and they forced Jeremiah and Baruch to go with them to Egypt where they all died. The prophet was clearly involved in the events about which he prophesied.

Although the prophets spoke from God they were not outsiders looking in. They were insiders—one with the people to whom they ministered and about whom they prophesied. They understood the messages they delivered and many of the implications.

Prophets Had Restricted Perspectives

When God spoke to and through His servants in predictive prophecy, God did not give them unlimited knowledge. Instead, they were confined within a divinely limited perspective.

This is particularly clear regarding the second coming of Christ. Most New Testament writers indicate they believed Christ would return during their own lifetimes. John in Revelation repeats this over and over. In Revelation 3:11, Christ declares, "I am coming at once" (without delay, *AT*). This appears three times in chapter 22—in verses 7, 12, and 20.

The New Testament writers believed Christ was returning to this earth to change it. Their belief was not a form of escapism. They believed that Christ's presence would break the hold that sin has on humanity.

But two thousand years have elapsed and Christ

still has not returned. This long interval does not, however, change the great issues that confront us. Each generation faces its own set of problems. How seriously we consider them shows whether God is real to us and whether we believe the climax of history is a genuine possibility.

Some predictions of the prophets dealt with the immediate future. Others looked down vast corridors of time, although the prophets themselves may not have realized that. They looked for the soon end of the present order and the beginning of the age to come. God limited their perspectives so that they and the people to whom they ministered would be God-centered rather than event-centered.

Prophets Spoke in the Languages and Thought Patterns of Their Own Day

The word choices of the prophets are colored by all their present and past experiences. The prophets spoke to their people in the thought and language patterns familiar to them.

To them, transportation meant horses, chariots, camels, boats. Armaments meant spears, shields, swords. Worship usually meant the Temple and sacrifices. The enemies of God were the Philistines, Moabites, Babylonians, and others.

When the prophets touched on events that are still in our day unfulfilled, their language is puzzling because the imagery is their own rather than ours. Thankfully, their emphasis is on God rather than on events. When events are placed in the foreground, people tend to put God in the background. This is a form of idolatry.

How do interpreters handle the language of predictive prophecy whose fulfillment is yet to come?

There have been three common methods.

Some interpreters expect literal fulfillment in all details. If the prophet mentions horses and bridles, some interpreters look for horses and bridles. If the prophet mentions shields, bucklers, bows and arrows, they believe that these are the weapons that will be used. This approach becomes a bit ludicrous when applied to today or to the future. It shows that the interpreter has forgotten the perspective of the prophets and the people to whom they ministered. The prophets talked to their people in the only language they all knew. When they thought of weapons, spears and shields came to mind.

Other interpreters apply a symbolic meaning to prophecy. These interpreters make predictive prophecy a picture of the hopes of the prophets for a better life. They apply a prophetic picture to the Christian church, covering part or all of the period from the beginning of the church to the New Jerusalem of Revelation 21 and 22.

Many interpreters think in terms of equivalents, analogy or correspondence. This is the approach preferred by the writers of this book. In this method, the chariots of the prophet's day will have an equivalent means of transportation at the time of the prophecy's fulfillment. The enemies of the people of God in one period are replaced by later enemies. The details of worship of God's people at an earlier period will be replaced by appropriate modes of worship during the period of fulfillment.

This principle can be illustrated by examining the prophecy in Ezekiel 40 to 48, where Ezekiel prophesied that worship of God would be restored. The prophet gave elaborate specifications as to the exact size of the Temple, floor plans, symbols to be used, the kind of sacrifices to be conducted there and their order, the garments the priests were to wear, whom they were to marry, what they were to teach the people, and how the land was to be divided among the people of Israel.

Where was Ezekiel when he received and delivered this prophecy? He and most other Jews were in exile in Babylon. There was no Temple at all, no priesthood, no ritual. Nor has Ezekiel's prophecy been fulfilled to the present day.

We cannot be sure what this means but we do know that the message brought by Ezekiel to his people encouraged them greatly. Those lonely, exiled people knew that the worship of God was not forever past. God would ultimately triumph and the knowledge of Him would never perish from the earth.

But what about this specific prophecy? Could Ezekiel's description of the worship of God by His people still be fulfilled in the day when Christ returns to bring the consummation of the age?

This is possible. But in the light of God's action in Jesus Christ, the fulfillment can hardly be literal. How could the true people of God return to the sacrifices that were abolished by the supreme sacrifice of Christ? The rituals of which Ezekiel spoke were but a shadow that was fulfilled in Christ. This is a place for the principle of equivalents.

The Temple, the ritual, and the priests involved in the ancient worship of God were meant to bring the Israelites into vital fellowship with God. The book of Hebrews says that with Christ as our High Priest, all older commandments regarding the priesthood are now annulled (Heb. 7:12-28). The things of which Ezekiel wrote were a shadow. Christ is the reality. The coming worship will exalt Jesus Christ.

The division of land among the twelve tribes of Israel, discussed by Ezekiel, may symbolize the perfect justice that Christ will bring when He returns. All past rivalries and inequities will disappear. God's people—now including both Jews and Gentiles—will be under Christ's command to bring in a whole new epoch.

Ezekiel used the language of his day and the worship forms familiar to his readers to make his message understandable to them. Today we have not only Ezekiel's language but also all of the New Testament. Yet we can still see only dimly the great glory yet to come!

Principles in Understanding Prophecy

Analyze the passage in terms of history, context, and its literal meaning. Learn all you can about the historical situation of the prophet and the people involved in his or her prophecy. Read carefully what precedes and what follows the particular passage being studied. Consult any parallel passages that may shed light. Don't be surprised to find that prophetic messages often are not arranged in any systematic order.

Note exactly to whom or to what the passage refers. Is the prophecy addressed to readers or hearers and is it also *about* those same readers or hearers? Are there any qualifications attached? Is it an "if these people do this thing, this will happen"?

If the prophecy has *forthtelling* (encouragement, admonition, warning) see how the people responded.

If the prophecy was *foretelling*, was it fulfilled? If it was fulfilled, study the writings that tell about the fulfillment. Some predictive prophecies, although referring to one specific event, may have additional applications. For example, Daniel 11 tells about the coming desecration of the Temple: "Forces from him shall appear and profane the temple and fortress, and shall take away the continual burnt offering. And they shall set up the abomination that makes desolate" (Dan. 11:31); there would be effort to totally eliminate Jewish forms of worship.

This prophecy was fulfilled in the terrible acts of Antiochus Epiphanes IV (170-168 BC) when he desecrated the Temple in Jerusalem, slaughtered thousands of Jews and finally set up a Greek altar to Zeus in the place where the altar for burnt offerings had once stood. He succeeded in shutting down Jewish worship for three years.

However, Jesus used the Daniel prophecy to refer to a different event when he spoke in Matthew 24:15, "So when you see the desolating sacrilege spoken of by the prophet Daniel, standing in the holy place (let the reader understand),. . ." Apparently Jesus was then referring to the fall of Jerusalem that would occur in AD 70.

Those same words may also describe a disruption in a pattern of worship in Palestine and Jerusalem at the time when Christ shall return. What the pattern of worship will then be, we do not now know.

Paul uses similar language to describe the man of sin, the final version of anti-Christ: "For that day will not come, unless the rebellion comes first, and the man of lawlessness is revealed, the son of perdition, who opposes and exalts himself against every so-called god or object of worship, so that he takes his seat in the temple of God, proclaiming himself to be God" (2 Thess. 2:3,4). Like Antiochus Epiphanes, the final version of anti-Christ will seek to set aside the established patterns of worship.

Multiple applications of prophetic language can and do occur. The prophetic message is real, but it is also elastic so that it can fit future changes. In this way we have an inkling about future opposition to God, but we do not "know times or seasons" (Acts 1:7).

Distinguish between direct and typological predictions, especially when the fulfillment of Old Testament prophecy is found in the New Testament.

Direct prediction means that an Old Testament prophecy is fulfilled solely in New Testament times. For example, Micah 5:2 states that Christ would be born in Bethlehem. The fulfillment is seen in Matthew 2:5,6.

A typological prediction is an Old Testament statement that referred to something in Old Testament times but had its highest application of meaning in the events, people, or message of the New Testament.

One such example of typology is seen in Zechariah 11:12,13, where the prophet Zechariah is acting as a shepherd for God's people. In the prophecy, Zechariah is "bought off" by the people for thirty pieces of silver, which he casts into the treasury of God's house. Matthew includes this passage (Matt. 26:15) in reference to the price paid to Judas for the betrayal of Jesus. Such typological predictions are common throughout the New Testament.

God's ultimate revelation of Himself in Christ colors all earlier revelations. We look at the Old Testament through the eyes of the Christian—not through the eyes of the Old Testament Jews. Christ, at the climax of His earthly ministry, spoke of one flock and one shepherd (John 10:16). We belong to this one flock, the church, Christ's Body. Jesus Christ forever broke down the barrier between Jews and Gentiles. The household of God is a living organism, tied to Jesus Christ. It includes believers from both the Old Covenant and the New Covenant. God has a great destiny for His people, since the New Covenant is an everlasting covenant (Heb. 13:20).

Apocalyptic imagery is difficult to handle. The term *apocalyptic* refers to those portions of the Bible in which the writer paints a dark picture of imminent disaster or cosmic cataclysm in which God destroys the ruling powers of evil and brings forth ultimate righteousness. There is usually a dark background with a bright ending. The books of Daniel, Zechariah, and Revelation have large sections of such material and other books have smaller amounts. In reading apocalyptic imagery we must follow the basic principles for all figurative language. Would our interpretation of this difficult imagery have made sense to the original readers? It is always better to say, "I don't know what this means," than to force a meaning that the imagery was not meant to carry. These problems will be discussed further in chapter 11 on the language of Genesis and Revelation.

What the first readers would have thought about a passage must be constantly considered. Occasionally the original readers (and perhaps even the writers) were wrong in what they concluded. For example, Paul and the early church obviously thought that the return of Christ would come within their own lifetimes. God chose to limit their perspectives in this regard, and the perspective of each Christian since then has been similarly limited. Knowing this, we have good reason not to be too dogmatic in our approach to passages of prophecy.

Questions for Discussion

1. Read Micah 6:1-16.
   a. Where did Micah get his message? (See Micah 3:8.)
   b. In a Bible dictionary or commentary, find out when Micah was written and to whom the prophecies were addressed.
   c. Which parts of this passage (Micah 6:1-16) are a call to a holy life (forthtelling) and which parts are *foretelling* the future?
   d. Do you think Micah 6:16b is apocalyptic language? Why or why not?
   e. In what ways do you think Micah's perspective was restricted? What part of the future did he see clearly? What part of the future did he not see clearly?

2. Read 2 Peter 3:1-18. Ask the following questions of this passage:
   a. What was the historical situation in which Peter wrote?
   b. What is the context of this passage? What comes before it and what comes after it? Does the context influence the meaning?
   c. To whom is the prophecy addressed? Is the message *about* these same people?
   d. Does it include any forthtelling (warning, call to holy life)?
   e. What parts are foretelling—prediction? Has the prediction been fulfilled?
   f. Does the passage have apocalyptic language?
   g. In what ways do you think Peter's vision of the future was limited? What did he see clearly? What did he not see clearly?

Chapter 11

The Language of Genesis and Revelation

Probably no parts of the Bible have aroused more emotion and disagreement than those regarding the creation of the world and its climax or culmination. Unfortunately, the heat of the discussions has rarely generated much light.

The basic question usually is: How literal or how figurative should be our interpretation of the Scriptures that deal with creation and with the end of time? The question is "*how* literal?" or "*how* figurative?" rather than "shall we be literal or shall we be figurative?" For the person who shouts the loudest for a "literal" interpretation nearly always has some figurative elements, and the one who espouses the "figurative" cause must base the meanings on literal elements.

For example, the story of the creation of man and woman as recorded in Genesis 1 and 2 says that God "breathed into his nostrils the breath of life; and man became a living being" (Gen. 2:7). It states that God walked "in the garden in the cool of the day" and "made for Adam and for his wife garments of skins, and clothed them" (Gen. 3:8,21).

A strictly literal approach to this picture would demand that God have lungs and legs so He could kneel beside the body of Adam and administer a kind of mouth-to-mouth respiration. It would demand a God who has feet with which to walk, and hands with which to sew. But Christ said that "God is spirit, and those who worship him must worship in spirit and truth" (John 4:24). Paul said, "[God] alone has immortality and dwells in unapproachable light, whom no man has ever seen or can see" (1 Tim. 6:16). How can both the account in Genesis and the words of the New Testament be "literally" true?

The interpreter who wants to make everything figurative is also caught in a bind. If Adam and Eve and the Fall are all figurative, is there any literal event, any historical occurrence, to which they point? If sin is a reality, how is it related to the story of Genesis? Has humanity always been at odds with God? Did people break off a harmonious relationship? These problems have concerned Christians for many generations.

Figurative Language Is Common in Jewish Thought

Careful study of the Bible shows that figurative language is deeply woven into the fabric of Jewish thought. Ancient people did not think or talk in abstractions or philosophical language as we often do. Early people constantly used figures of speech drawn from their everyday agricultural and pastoral lives.

In talking about God, biblical writers frequently used figures of speech called anthropomorphisms—

physical qualities of humans used to describe God. The writer of Genesis no doubt knew that God did not have hands or feet or lungs. But he also knew that God had created Adam in a sense similar to that in which a potter forms or molds a container, and that God made it possible for Adam to breathe or live. The writer knew that God cares for the physical needs of people in the sense that a tailor clothes people. He knew that Adam and Eve could commune with God somewhat as a person talks to another person in a garden.[1]

To say that such language is figurative does not mean that the event it is describing is imaginary. Figurative language may be the most accurate way to convey what is real, abiding, and certain. Any words used to describe events that took place or will take place in a sphere of existence that no human has observed is by its very nature figurative. No human was present at creation; climax is yet to take place. Any account of these events would have to be written in language based on the known or experienced phenomena of the writer. How else could any meaning be conveyed?

Creation Account Is Prescientific

The language of the creation account is prescientific and is directed to those who knew nothing of the vastness of space, the world of the microscope, or the intricacies of physical organisms. Most people still know little about these things. Any pride in our superior scientific knowledge is ridiculous when we consider the vast areas about which science still knows little or nothing.

If the Bible had been written in the scientific language of our day it would have been meaningless to all who preceded us and it would be meaningless to generations yet to come who will develop vocabulary and concepts unknown to us. The accounts could be useful only if written within the framework and cosmology of people of that day. It is popular prescientific language.

God as the Ultimate Cause

In dealing with passages about creation or climax we must note that the writers did not discuss "how." They did not concern themselves with secondary causes and effects but focused on God as the ultimate cause.

Unfortunately, we keep asking *how* God did this or that, and *how* God will accomplish something in the future, rather than giving our primary attention to the clearly stated fact that God did or will do it.

Events Are Not Always Chronological

Biblical narratives about creation are written in the style and outlook of ancient people. This means, among other things, that events are not necessarily recounted in chronological order. This is true of many parts of the Old Testament. In the book of Jeremiah the writer starts with events during the reign of one king, then moves to another king, and then comes back to the first king. Chronology was not as important to ancient writers as it is to us.

Poetic sequence, subject matter, logic, or some other factor often determined the arrangement rather than chronology. Not understanding this, even a grade-school child may be confused by the Genesis account in which light was created on the "first day" while the sun was not made until the "fourth day."

Certain Numbers Had Symbolic Meaning

Certain symbolic numbers had great importance to ancient people. The number seven appears symbolically in the writings not only of the Hebrews but of all Semites. It seems to signify a fullness or totality. To the Hebrews it symbolized a totality designed and ordained by God.

The number seven played quite an important part in the religious ritual of Hebrews and in their ways of recounting history. In Genesis 10, the names in the generations of Noah total seventy—a "full" picture of the nations of the world. In Numbers 11:16, Moses appoints seventy elders over the people of Israel. In Exodus 1:5 we are told that "all the offspring of Jacob were seventy persons." In Genesis 4:24 Cain was avenged sevenfold and Lamach seventy times seven.

The story of a boy who was brought back to life by Elisha is recounted in 2 Kings 4:35. It says the boy sneezed seven times—an indication that life had fully returned.

The use of seven and its multiples is also prominent in the New Testament. The story of the seven brothers who successively married the same woman is obviously meant to give Jesus the idea of an extensive series (Matt. 22:23-32).

In Matthew 1, the genealogy of Joseph lists three series of fourteen generations. Matthew's selection does not coincide with Old Testament genealogies, but Matthew apparently chose names to be included in his genealogy so that they would come out in a series of three fourteens. This may have been a memory device, or a desire to use a multiple of seven, or a combination of both.

Jesus told of the man who was to be forgiven not

seven times, but seventy times seven—continually and fully forgiven. In Luke 10:1, Jesus sent out seventy disciples.

Symbolic use of the number seven comes to much fuller play in the book of Revelation. The book is addressed to seven churches (1:4); and speaks of seven spirits before God's throne (1:4); seven lampstands (1:12); seven stars (1:16); seven seals (5:1); seven trumpets and seven angels (8:2); seven thunders (10:3); seven heads and seven crowns (12:3; 13:1; 17:3); seven bowls of wrath (16:1); a lamb that has seven horns and seven eyes (5:6). The beast (dragon) has seven heads (12:3)—perhaps to indicate the full development of the forces hostile to God.

Why did the number seven gain such significance? We cannot be sure, of course, but perhaps seven appeared significant to ancient people in their then observable cosmos and its order. Ancient people may have found their first basis of reckoning and dividing time by observing the four phases of the moon in seven-day periods. Thus a "week" may have been their first measurable unit of time beyond the sunrise and sunset that marked a day.

How natural, then, for the writer of Genesis to use a seven-day literary framework as his symbolic unit to describe the completion of a cataclysmic, significant event! The early readers or listeners of the account likely understood the use of this literary framework far better than readers of more recent generations—especially of Western civilization.

This use of a seven-day literary framework is also found in early literature outside the Bible. The Canaanites had a story about a palace to their god Baal that was erected in seven days—although it would have been impossible for a palace to be constructed with primitive building methods in seven days. It was simply a number indicating the completion of an important event that took an indefinite period of time.

Ancient people had patterns of thought and ways of expressing ideas that were very different from twentieth-century Western modes. Unless we struggle to understand the early framework, culture, and thought pattern, we may grossly misinterpret what these ancient writings are saying.

Creation Story in a Framework of Seven Days

The Genesis account of creation uses a Hebrew framework of seven days. The week is divided into two three-day periods.

Genesis 1:2 describes the earth as "without form and void." The Hebrew phrase is *tohu wa-bohu*. The phrase itself has a poetic ring. *Tohu* means unformed and *bohu* means empty or unfilled.

During the first half (three days) of the six-day work week, God remedied the "formless" aspect of the earth by acts of dividing. On the first "day" He divided the light from darkness. On the second "day" God divided the "lower waters" from the "upper waters." (The ancients thought of the "firmament" or "heavens" not as space but as a solid substance, so that the "firmament" formed a sort of canopy over the earth. Today we call this atmosphere.) On the third "day" God divided the lower waters from the dry land and also covered the earth with vegetation.

In the last three "days" of work God "filled" the emptiness or void of the earth, according to the writer of Genesis. The work of these last three days follows the same pattern as that of the first three.

On the fourth "day" God created the sun, moon,

and stars. This corresponds to the first day's activity of separating light from darkness.

The fifth "day" God filled the "lower waters" with fish and sea creatures, and the "upper waters" (atmosphere) with birds. The dividing of the "upper and lower waters" had been made on the second "day."

On the sixth "day" God filled the dry land that had been "formed" on the third day. On it God placed animals and people and told Adam and Eve that the food was for them and the animals.

Day	God *forms* by dividing	Day	God *fills* by making
1	light from darkness	4	sun, moon, stars
2	upper waters from lower waters	5	fish and birds
3	dry land from seas (plus creation of vegetation as food for those who would "fill" it)	6	animals and man

As we look at the Genesis account from this perspective, it appears that it is written within a literary framework rather than in a chronological or scientific framework. This in no way lessens the great truth the creation account teaches.

The Genesis account corrects common philosophical and theological errors.

First: it teaches clearly that God and nature are not the same. The pantheist gains no support from Genesis. It teaches that God is above and separate from the universe. He is the Creator.

Second, Genesis teaches that there is *one* God. God is not one among many.

Third, Genesis teaches that God is good and that everything He made was good.

Fourth, Genesis teaches that God moved in an orderly way from a chaotic situation to one of form and beauty. Creation did not do this by itself.

Vocabulary of Creation and Climax

The Hebrew language was highly pictorial, built on the agricultural and pastoral life of the people. The early Hebrews, like every generation before or since, were largely enclosed within their own mode of life. Their language reflected that mode. Ideas can be portrayed only in language known to the writers or speakers. Therefore, language based on the biblical writers' experiences had to be used to describe the distant past, the distant future and the eternal realities as they understood them.

The biblical picture of heaven is expressed in terms of the palaces and riches of earthly potentates. Gold, jewels, rich robes, crowns, thrones signified the epitome of splendor on earth. Naturally, the biblical writers used such terms to describe the splendors of heaven. The original readers may have been more aware of the symbolic nature of the language than today's readers are.

To illustrate the language problems involved in the creation and climax accounts, let us examine Genesis 2:7,8. "Then the Lord God formed man of dust from the ground, and breathed into his nostrils the breath of life; and man became a living being. And the Lord God planted a garden in Eden, in the east; and there he put the man whom he had formed."

How God "formed." The verb used here for "formed" is the Hebrew word *yatzar*, which means to form or fashion. The participle (forming) is used in Jeremiah 18:4-6 to describe a potter forming a vessel. The potter is spoken of as the one forming. When this idea is applied to God, the figurative meaning is immediately apparent. God does not have hands to handle clay as the potter does. But this language gives a more personal feeling than the more abstract word "create." We sense the personal involvement of God as the one forming.

What did God "form" or "mold"? In Genesis 2:7,8, He formed or molded man. In Genesis 2:19, the same word is used of animals. "So out of the ground the Lord God *formed* every beast of the field and every bird of the air" (italics added).

Apparently God used the same materials to form man, birds, and animals—"out of the ground." This seems to indicate what common sense and science have long confirmed—that the physical elements of people, birds, and beasts have a common base.

This common base has been a great boon to medical science. It makes it possible, for example, for a person with diabetes to use insulin from a cow or a pig, so that such a person can live a full and useful life.

After death, man, beasts and birds all return to "dust" as Genesis 3:19 states with remarkable simplicity: "You are dust, and to dust you shall return."

In Isaiah 44:1,2, a figure of speech involving *yatzar* (to form) shows that such forming may have involved a process.

"But now hear, O Jacob my servant, Israel whom I have chosen!

Thus says the Lord who made you,

who formed you from the womb and will
help you."

The opening words show that the passage refers
to the nation Israel. The figure of speech is that of an
infant growing in its mother's womb, and the figure
is compared to God's forming of the people of Israel.
Both the figure of speech (the growth of the infant in
the uterus) and the development of Israel indicate
that this "forming" was a process that continued over
a period of time. In fact, in Isaiah's time God was still
forming or fashioning the nation even though more
than a thousand years had passed since God had first
called Abraham to be the father of a great multitude.

In Isaiah 43:1, the verb *barah* (to create) is used
as a synonym for the verb *yatzar* (to form) in a typical
case of Hebrew poetic parallelism.

"But now thus says the	
Lord	*literal*
he who created you,	"the one creating you,
O Jacob;	O Jacob;
he who formed you,	the one forming you,
O Israel."	O Israel."

The "creation" of Jacob (the nation Israel) was
obviously no instantaneous act involving making
something out of nothing. The active participle in
Hebrew, which is used here, *boracká*, indicates a
person or thing conceived of as being in continual
uninterrupted exercise of an activity.[2]

God is pictured both as Creator and Sustainer of
the universe in Jeremiah 10:12,13, where the active
Hebrew participle makes clear His activity: "It is he
who made [literally, 'was making'] the earth by his
power, who established [literally, 'was establishing']
the world by his wisdom, and by his understanding
stretched out the heavens.

When he utters his voice there is a tumult
of waters in the heavens,
and he makes the mist rise from the ends of
the earth.
He makes lightnings for the rain,
and he brings forth [literally, 'is bringing
    forth'] the wind from his storehouses."

These passages and others like them show that God is personally involved not only in the creation of the world but also in its daily operation. The creation of the world involved process, and God continues the process of its daily operation. Yet God's personal involvement in the thunderstorm does not mean that secondary causes, such as high pressure centers, are not at work.

How God "Breathed"

The terms "breathed" and "breath of life" also appear in Genesis 2:7. "Then the Lord God formed man of dust from the ground, and *breathed* into his nostrils the *breath* of life; and man became a living being" (italics added).

Breath is used often in the Bible to symoblize or indicate a living creature. For example, Job maintains that he will not be guilty of falsehood nor will he utter deceit as long as his *breath* is in him (Job 27:3,4).

God's "breathing" into man the breath of life obviously is figurative language for giving life to Adam.

Who Is a "Living Being"?

The term "living being" from the Hebrew word *nefesh chayyah* refers to Adam in Genesis 2:7. However, it is also used in Genesis 2:19 to refer to ani-

mals. "And whatever the man called every living creature [*nefesh chayyah*] that was its name."

The same term appears in Genesis 1:20,21,24,30
in describing the fish, birds, and animals. It appears
in Genesis 9:12,15 in reference to the covenant that
God made with Noah and his sons and with "every living creature."

Some people believe the term "living being" in
Genesis 2:7 refers to man's eternal soul, but a study
of the use of the word in other contexts rules this
out—unless one is willing to say that every fish, bird,
and animal also has an eternal soul.

Actually, the description of man as a "living being"
in Genesis 2:7 shows his likeness to other living
things rather than his differences from them. The
fact that only man and woman were made "in the
image of God" makes them different from all other
creatures. "So God created man in his own image, in
the image of God he created him; male and female he
created them. And God blessed them, and God said to
them, 'Be fruitful and multiply, and fill the earth and
subdue it; and have dominion over the fish of the sea
and over the birds of the air and over every living
thing that moves upon the earth' " (Gen. 1:27,28).

At least part of being made "in the image of God"
involves the responsibility of men and women to
properly use the earth's resources. The results of sin
can be clearly seen in what we have done with our
"dominion." When we are fully conformed to Christ,
then God's image will be restored in us. Our intellect,
emotions, will, plans, purpose and activities will be
in complete harmony with God's will.

Language of Final Judgment and Destiny
When people ask, "Do you believe in a literal

heaven and hell?" we are again confronted with the meaning of "literal." If the question is phrased, "Do you believe in the reality of heaven and hell?" it takes on a different meaning.

The language describing heaven and hell are examples of truth and reality being conveyed by figures of speech.

"Then I saw a great white throne and him who sat upon it; from his presence earth and sky fled away, and no place was found for them. And I saw the dead, great and small, standing before the throne, and books were opened. Also another book was opened, which is the book of life. And the dead were judged by what was written in the books, by what they had done. And the sea gave up the dead in it, Death and Hades gave up the dead in them, and all were judged by what they had done. Then Death and Hades were thrown into the lake of fire" (Rev. 20:11-14).

No one can read all of this passage with a strictly literal approach. The very terms Death and Hades are personified or they could not be "thrown into the lake of fire." Earth and sky are also personified, for they "flee away."

The descriptions of God use anthropomorphisms. He is described with the qualities of humans. He is seated upon a "throne." Heaven and earth flee from His "face." Yet this figurative language is effective in conveying dramatic truths: God is a personal being of majesty and power—not an abstract force.

The next sentence pictures the dead—the small and great—standing before the throne of God. The books are opened. This figure of speech is a bit archaic in modern times. A writer today would probably use a picture of recall on a word processor. Either way, the truth comes through that God knows the doings of people and their destiny. There is judgment after death and we will have to answer to God for what we are, what we have thought, and what we have done. Could this have been made so clear and forceful *without* figurative language?

Death in the New Testament is called the last enemy to be abolished (see 1 Cor. 15:26,54,55). Death is pictured as separation of a person from his or her body (2 Cor. 5:6-8; Phil. 1:21-24).

The Christian, though separated from his or her body, is in the presence of the Lord. Hades is pictured as the place of the dead and also as a place of punishment (Luke 16:23). The non-Christian in Hades is separated from his or her body *and* from God. Physical death is the only separation a Christian can experience, but for the one who rejects Jesus Christ, physical death is a prelude to a total separation from God.

The reality of punishment leaps through the figurative language of Revelation. Ultimate separation from God is described here as the second death or the lake of fire. This dramatic language shows the wretchedness of being banished from the presence of God.

Understanding the Language of Creation and Climax

Figurative language is the only way to convey realities that lie beyond human experience. Now we know only in part, but without such language our ignorance would be total. Though our knowledge may be small it is extremely valuable. *It is all we need to know* to live richly and meaningfully with God and with each other.

The realities described by the language of crea-

tion and climax are important. We are deeply involved in the results of creation and will be active participants in the judgment, blessing, or punishment of life after death.

The truths of Scripture regarding creation and climax are not given to satisfy our scientific curiosity nor as a horoscope to the future. What we do not know has sometimes become a battleground among Christians so that we lose sight of what we do know. The basic message of creation and climax is urgent and must be heard.

The kind of language employed ought to increase our awareness of how great God is. We dare not diminish God to our size.

Questions for Discussion

1. Read Isaiah 45:9-12,18.
   a. What figures of speech do you find in this portion?
   b. What truth does each figure express?
   c. How many different words for "create" do you find? What enriched meanings do these words give?
2. Read Daniel 7:9,10,13,14.
   a. List all the figures of speech *about God* in this section.
   b. How do these figures of speech help to make God real to you?
   c. Do any of these word pictures tend to *confuse* your concept of God or your concept of the end of the age?

If any of them tend to confuse your ideas, do you think our own thought patterns make these figures difficult for us? Do you think the original readers had the same problems? Why or why not?

Notes

1. Some of the material in this chapter is adapted from writings of Ronald Youngblood, professor of Old Testament and Semitic Languages, Bethel Theological Seminary, San Diego Campus. For fuller discussion, see Youngblood's *How It All Began* (Ventura, CA: Regal Books, 1980).

2. *Gesenius' Hebrew Grammar*, edited and enlarged by Kautzsch and Cowley (Oxford: Oxford University Press, 1910), paragraph 116a.

Chapter 12

Understanding the Poetry of the Bible

For reasons that most of us cannot explain, poetry often seems to reach deeply into our souls. Analysis of the mechanics of poetry can never tell us why some poems impress us so deeply.

C.S. Lewis observed that "only poetry can speak low enough to catch the faint murmur of the mind."[1]

Wordsworth said that poetry is "the overflow of spontaneous emotion recollected in tranquility."[2]

Poetry enlists the artist in the most blundering of us and for a few moments permits us to escape the cramped quarters of our own outlook. It opens our eyes, minds, and feelings to a rich world of reality to which most of us pay only fleeting visits.

Since poetry seems to reach into the vary marrow of our bones, it is not surprising that much of the Bible is in poetry. This is especially true of the Old Testament, where Hebrews who felt deeply poured out their souls in poetry that still penetrates our inner beings many centuries later.

Those who use the *King James Version* or the

American Standard Version of 1901 or *The Living Bible* may not be aware of how extensive poetry is in the Old Testament, because the poetic sections are not printed in a form that permits us to recognize them as poetry. The *Revised Standard Version*, the *New International Version* and many of the other newer versions do print poetry as poetry. The following Old Testament books are all or nearly all in poetry:

Psalms	Lamentations
Proverbs	Amos
Job	Obadiah
Song of Solomon	Micah
Isaiah	Nahum
Jeremiah	Habakkuk
Joel	Zephaniah

Other books have extensive sections of poetry, including Ecclesiastes and Zechariah.

Read Poetry with a Poetic Frame of Mind

Regardless of how limited is our own poetic sense or our ability to produce poetry, we all know that we approach poetry with a different frame of mind than we use with prose. We come prepared with our imaginations sharpened, our rhythmic senses ready to carry us along the swells and recesses. We are prepared for figures of speech, and we know better than to read poetry with a strictly literal approach. When we see something written in poetic form, our minds automatically prepare themselves to receive poetry.

This frame of mind is important as we study the poetic sections of the Old Testament. One of the tragedies of translations that do not print poetry as poetry is that the reader does not know when to make the mental and emotional transition to poetry.

Hebrew Poetic Form Is Different

Hebrew poetry is not like Western poetry. Much modern poetry and some ancient poetry is based on a balance of sound—phonetic rhythm. Nursery rhymes are a simple form of this balance of sound. Our more sophisticated poetry often does not incorporate rhyme at all, but it usually does have a certain balance of rhythm.

But Hebrew and Akkadian poetry (as well as Egyptian and Chinese) consists of a balance of thought rather than a balance of sound. It has a rhythm of *logic*. The poetry follows one idea by another line of thought parallel to the first. A verse consists of at least two parts in which the second part has a thought that is parallel to the first. This *parallelism* is the main feature of Hebrew poetry.

Although two lines usually constitute a verse, there are also three- four- and even five-line verses in Hebrew poetry. The balance of thought in these lines usually involves a certain number of stressed units in each line. In the most common two-line verses, there are often three stressed units in each line. Look at Psalm 103:10 (literal translation):

Not-according-to-our-sins / did-he-act / toward-us;
Not-according-to-our-iniquities / did-he-deal-fully / against-us.

This parallelism in which the second line repeats the same ideas as the first is the most common type and is known as *synonymous parallelism*.

The poetic Hebrews did not limit themselves to one form. They also used *contrasting parallelism* in which the second line expresses a thought in sharp contrast to that of the first line. Proverbs 15:1 is an example (literal translation):

A-gentle-answer / turns-away / rage,
But-word-that-hurts / stirs-up / anger.

There is also *parallelism of emblems*. In this form, one line uses a figurative statement and the other line a more literal one, as in Psalm 42:1 (literal translation):

As-a-hart / longs / for-flowing-streams,
So-my-soul / longs / for-thee-O-God.

Another fascinating variation in Hebrew poetry is *stair-like parallelism*. In this form a part of the first line is repeated while newer elements build up to a climax. This is seen in Psalm 29:1,2:

Ascribe / to-the-Lord / O-heavenly-beings,
ascribe / to-the-Lord / glory-and-strength.
Ascribe / to-the-Lord / the-glory-of-his-name.

The Hebrew poets were not slaves to any form. We often find their parallelism incomplete with some units missing. This is their kind of "free verse." In the illustration just given, the third unit of the first line is not really parallel to the third unit of the second and third lines. Sometimes incomplete parallelism is compensated for by adding other stressed units that are not parallel in thought, as in Psalm 103:15 (literal translation):

As-for-man / his-days / are-as-the-green-grass
As-the-flowers-of-the-field / so / he-blossoms.

Whether the parallelism is complete or not, the reader who knows he is reading poetry is carried along as the writers pour forth their anguish, their joys, their expectations from God, their concerns for themselves and their people.

Stanzas in Hebrew Poetry

For the past one hundred years, there has been prolonged discussion and some disagreement among scholars as to how Hebrew poetry is grouped to form stanzas. There are differences of opinion where the author has not clearly indicated his intention by some Hebrew device. There were two devices which, when used, made the intention of the author clear.

Sometimes the Hebrews used a *recurring refrain* to indicate the opening or closing of a stanza. In Psalm 136, the words "for his steadfast love endures for ever" recurs after every line. However, this demands an intolerable number of stanzas, so editors have grouped the ideas together to form longer stanzas. Sometimes ideas are clearly grouped, and this kind of stanza division then becomes easy.

Some Hebrew poets gave a sure indication of stanzas by use of an *acrostic*. In this device, a group of lines begins with the first letter of the Hebrew alphabet, followed by the next letter for the next group. This accounts for the length of Psalm 119 where the author used eight consecutive lines beginning with the first letter of the Hebrew alphabet, followed by eight lines beginning with the second letter, eight lines with the third, and so on through the twenty-two letters of the Hebrew alphabet.

Other acrostic poems are found in Psalms 25, 35, and 145, where each two-line verse begins with consecutive letters of the Hebrew alphabet. The beautiful Lamentations chapters 1,2,3, and 4 are based on a similar acrostic. Although the acrostic idea seems artificial and self-limiting to us, the Hebrew poets were apparently able to rise above such limitations, for few passages are more picturesque than Lamentations 1 to 4.

The majority of Hebrew poetry does not have such clear indications of stanzas, however, and in these cases the poetic paragraphing (stanzas) of the translators must guide us. Unless we pay attention to these smaller units, we may not be able to understand the whole.

Poetry Is Personal

Poetry is essentially a personal experience—both to the writer and to the reader. We dare not become absorbed in the mechanics of it. We should concentrate rather on the personal quality of the poetry, especially in the Psalms, for this is what attracts so many day after day. The reader can enter into the rich experiences of the poet and find there that the language of the poet expresses his own longings, hopes, disappointments and trials.

Most readers would find it a worthy experience to read through the book of Lamentations at a single sitting. The poet has shared the calamity of his own people and he expresses not only his own sorrows and sufferings but also the collective sorrow and suffering of his people. Out of deep pessimism he also recounts their only hope in Lamentations 3:22,23 (literal translation):

> It is the steadfast hope of Jehovah,
> that we do not come to an end;
> that his mercies do not fail.
> They are new every morning.
> Great is Thy faithfulness.

The poet finds that he can face reality because he stands face to face with God.

Poetry Is Rich in Imagery

By its very nature, poetry lends itself to figurative language. The Hebrews were masters of figurative language even in prose, and in poetry their intense creativity in figurative language had full reign. The passage in Isaiah 1:2,3 illustrates this:

Hear, O heavens, and give ear, O earth;
for the Lord has spoken:
"Sons have I reared and brought up,
but they have rebelled against me.
The ox knows its owner,
and the ass its master's crib;
but Israel does not know,
my people do not understand."

Here a personified heaven and earth are asked to listen to the charge of the Lord. The sons whom He has reared have rebelled against Him. The ox and ass know their master, but not so God's people. The passage (vv. 5,6) goes on to describe Israel as one in whom

The whole head is sick,
and the whole heart faint.
From the sole of the foot to the head,
there is no soundness in it,
but bruises and sores
and bleeding wounds;
they are not pressed out, or bound up,
or softened with oil.

The nation of Israel is personified as a sick and bruised person.

The entire chapter is rich in imagery, all taken from the daily life of the people. Most of it is taken from their agrarian economy, and although we no longer live in this kind of society, the imagery still speaks strongly to us.

Understanding Poetry in Psalms

If possible, try to find the historical occasion for the particular psalm. The content of the psalm and the individual psalm title often give clues. A good commentary may help. However, it is better to admit ignorance of the particular context than to assign it arbitrarily to a particular historical occasion if there is not enough evidence to justify such an assignment.

Try to understand the attitude, the outlook, the spiritual and psychological mood of the poet when he composed the psalm. John Calvin called the Psalms, "an anatomy of all parts of the soul."[3]

In dealing with the imprecatory psalms (those in which the psalmist hurls curses at his enemies) such as Psalm 109:6-20 and Psalm 137:7-9, *regard such passages as poetic expressions of persons who were incensed at the tyranny of evil.* They are so colored by their sense of being wronged or by their outrage at the blasphemy committed that they forget to leave judgment to God. These psalms show what injustice and evil can do even to a good man. For further discussion of these Psalms see C.S. Lewis, *Reflections on the Psalms.*[4]

In the messianic psalms (2, 16, 22, 40, 45, 69, 72, 98, 110 and others), *note the elements that applied to the time of the writer as well as to the time of Christ.* Consider why certain factors, because of what they involve, could only belong in the highest degree to the Messiah. The beauty of expression in these psalms must be appreciated in terms of the historical perspective at the time of their writing.

Observe the poet's basic convictions about God. The poet returns to these convictions when he feels the mounting pressures of life.

Understanding Poetry in Proverbs

Proverbs is a group of maxims or short sagacious sayings that were taken from everyday life and handed down from one generation to another. The fact that these sayings were handed down in poetic form is another indication of the artistic temperament of the Hebrew people.

The proverbs deal with problems of personal life, of interpersonal relationships, of our relationship with God, of moral principles, of attitude toward possessions, and other topics.

Unlike us, the Hebrews made no distinction between what is secular and what is sacred. They believed that God was the God of the whole earth who exercised authority in every aspect of life.

Although we may classify the proverbs as to subject matter, *we should not think of some as "religious" and others as "nonreligious."* This is foreign to the thinking of the Hebrew people from whom these proverbs come.

Some proverbs are obscure. Occasionally the context may shed some light on the meaning because some proverbs are grouped together so that a common or parallel theme is developed. If the obscurity cannot be removed, admit it freely and center attention on the sections that *can* be understood. Watch for short figures of speech in Proverbs and apply the principles for figurative language.

Job—the Greatest Old Testament Poetry

The prologue and epilogue of Job are in prose. The remainder of the book is poetry. The prologue (Job 1:1—2:13) gives the setting of the book. It tells about the faithfulness of Job, the council in the court of heaven, the misfortunes of Job, and the visit of his three friends. The epilogue (Job 42:7-17) describes the restoration of Job.

The remaining 40 chapters of Job are written in poetry. The poet wrestles with the basic questions of all people: What is the meaning of life? How does a person of faith react to suffering? How can a person approach God? What is the meaning of faith, of integrity, of purpose? Such questions all point to the reality of God, even though we do not have the answers to life's enigmas.

Job is probably the greatest poetry in the Old Testament. The writer is eloquent, versatile, vigorous, and concise. To get the most out of studying Job, consider the following suggestions.

Study the complete utterances of the main characters: Job, Eliphaz, Bildad, Zophar, and Elihu. Look for the basic assumptions of each and evaluate their arguments with these in mind.

Study the declarations of God. Consider the emphasis on Job's ignorance and see how this is related to the self-confidence of the other characters.

Recognize the basic questions and look for the answers that are given to them. We are tempted to look for answers to questions that the author did not discuss and then we are annoyed by his lack of answers to our chosen questions! Notice that only certain aspects of questions are discussed. On these particular aspects there is a good deal of illumination. This illumination is of the searchlight variety, however, with many facets of the topic still in the dark.

Job himself had to find out that it was *not* information he needed so much as he needed God Himself: "I have heard of thee by the hearing of the ear: but now mine eye seeth thee" (Job 42:5, *KJV*).

Understanding Poetry in the Prophets

Try to see the prophet as a person as well as a poet.

Use the standard principles of studying context, history, and culture to see the specific situation out of which the poetry arose.

Note how the poetic imagery and the personal dimension of the prophet speak to us, enabling us to enter into his or her situation and to share his or her message from God.

Questions for Discussion

Read Isaiah 5:1-30. Use a translation that prints poetry as poetry. Do NOT use King James, American Standard, or Living Bible.

1. Read all the way through aloud, trying to feel the poetic flow of words and ideas in the picturesque language of this literary form. (If you are studying in a group, read in unison if you have the same version, or have one person read aloud as the rest listen. Or have all read aloud their own versions at the same time—Chinese fashion! Tell them to concentrate on the sound of their own voices and the poetic flow of words.)

2. Notice how the translators divided the poetry into stanzas. Write in the margin of your Bible the one main idea in each stanza.

3. Study the parallelism of the poetry.

    a. In verses 20 to 23, notice the synonymous parallelism—lines where the same idea is repeated two or three times in different words. Does the repetition intensify the idea?

    b. Notice the contrasting parallelism in verses 15 and 16, followed by synonymous parallelism in verse 17.

    c. Find the parallelism of symbols in verses 5 to 7. (Verses 5 and 6 give figures of speech, while verse 7 uses a more literal meaning.)

    d. Find the four-step synonymous parallelism in verse 6 and the contrasting parallelism in verse 7.

4. What personal elements do you find in verses 1 to 30 about which you can say, "Yes, I know that from experience"?

5. In verses 24 to 30, find two or three figures of speech (metaphors, similes, personifications) that add strength to the poetry.

6. Do you think this would have been more effective as a sermon instead of poetry?

Notes

1. C.S. Lewis, *Letters to Malcolm*. (New York: Harcourt Brace Jovanovich, Inc., 1963), p. 112.

2. William Wordsworth, *Lyrical Ballads*, 2nd ed. (New York: Oxford University Press, 1969), preface.

3. John Calvin, *Commentary on the Book of Psalms* (1845), I, xxxxvi.

4. C.S. Lewis, "The Cursings," *Reflections on the Psalms*. (New York: Harcourt Brace Jovanovich, Inc., 1958), pp. 20-33.

Chapter 13

How Do We Build Doctrine and Theology?

No area of the Christian church stands more in need of renewal and spiritual awakening than that of doctrinal teaching or theology. Unfortunately, many people think of doctrine or theology as some boring, abstract, philosophical approach to Christianity that has no application to their daily lives or which requires a mastery of technical theological terminology.

This is a misunderstanding. Doctrine and theology affect every facet of our lives and do not demand theological jargon. Our choices and attitudes are determined largely by our theology, whether we realize it or not. For this reason it is crucial that our theology be sound and truly biblical.

The word "doctrine" comes from the Greek word *didaskalia* which means "teaching." It refers both to the act of teaching and to what is taught (*the* teaching). The word *Torah* or *law* in Hebrew also means "teaching." Therefore the "law of the Lord" means basically the "teaching of the Lord."

The suffix *ology* means a branch or body of learning. Thus, biology refers to a body of learning about organic life. Theology refers to learning or teaching about God. Thus theology and doctrine mean basically the same thing.

In our use of the words *doctrine* or *theology* today, we often refer to a more narrow meaning, usually a group of specific truths about God and our relationship to God. We study a doctrine or theology of sin (known as *harmartology*), of salvation (known as *soteriology*), of Christ (known as *Christology*), or things yet to come (known as *eschatology*).

Such study ought to have one main purpose: to make it easier for these truths to become a part of our lives. To have value, doctrine must be both "learned" and "walked."

The Bible itself does not teach doctrine in the narrow sense of an organized system of thought. The Bible is basically a "case history" of God's dealings with people and their responses to Him. God dealt with people in terms of their own lives, their historical situations. The Old Testament regulations that appear in Exodus and Deuteronomy were given by God for the Israelites as they were leaving hundreds of years of slavery in Egypt and embarking on a new way of life as a nation. The letters of the New Testament were written to specific churches or individuals in historical situations that may have been similar to or different from our situations. They are not books of doctrine as such.

But from these books and all others in the Old and New Testaments, we can learn about God and His plans and purposes for people of that day and of our day. From such study we formulate our doctrine or theology on which we base our daily decisions and beliefs.

One fact needs to be emphasized and reemphasized: doctrinal truth is only partial. God has not chosen to reveal everything we would like to know. Paul makes this very clear in 1 Corinthians 13:12: "For now we see in a mirror dimly, but then face to face. Now I know in part; then I shall understand fully, even as I have been fully understood."

Sometimes theologians are tempted to formulate doctrine on the basis of what they think God *should* do rather than limiting themselves to what the Scriptures actually say. The Bible does not answer all our questions. Since it is hard to live with unanswered questions, we are sometimes tempted to fill in the unknowns with our own wishful thinking.

Such a route can have tragic consequences as the Apostle Peter found out in the story recounted in Mark 8:27-33. Jesus asked the disciples, "Who do people say I am?" Peter gave his personal opinion and it was the right answer, "You are the Christ" (vv. 27,29, *NIV*).

Jesus then told the disciples that He must go to Jerusalem to suffer and be killed. Peter could not fit that teaching into his own Jewish theology that said that the Messiah would restore the kingdom to Israel and deliver Israel from the rule of Rome. So Peter took Christ aside and began to rebuke Him for saying such things.

Jesus gave Peter one of the strongest rebukes recorded in the New Testament. "Get behind me, Satan! For you are not on the side of God, but of men" (v. 33, *RSV*).

We must be careful not to follow Peter's route of trying to structure God's ways in terms of what we think God should do or should have done. In taking such care, we may have to be satisfied with fewer absolute answers to hard questions and leave more room for honest differences of opinion among Christians.

Two Kinds of Theology

Among biblical scholars, there are two branches of theology. One is known as biblical theology and the other as systematic theology. Both must be based on the Bible and both are essential to a solid understanding of the Scriptures.

Biblical theology emphasizes history. Biblical theology deals with how the historical frameworks of the Old and New Testaments influence their teachings. Every teaching of the Bible came into a particular historical situation. Biblical theologians try to see how a particular teaching was influenced by its historical situation and how the message from God was particularly suited to the needs of people in that situation. Biblical theology could more properly be called the historical theology of the Old Testament and the historical theology of the New Testament.

For example, 1, 2, and 3 John were written late in the first century when the teachings of gnosticism were appearing. The gnostics taught that only "spirit" was good and that "matter" was essentially evil. For this reason, the gnostics despised the physical body, believing it was evil because it was material.

The influence of this teaching can be seen in 1 John 4:2,3, where the writer states, "Every spirit which confesses that Jesus Christ has come *in the flesh* is of God, and every spirit which does not confess Jesus Christ is not of God" (italics added).

The same idea appears in John 1:14: "And the Word became flesh and dwelt among us, full of grace and truth; we have beheld his glory, glory as of the only Son from the Father." John probably taught this in response to the gnostic teaching which denied that Christ truly became flesh.

Another example of doctrinal teaching in response to an historical situation appears in Hebrews 1. Biblical theologians point out that the original readers of this letter were enamored with angels. Thus the writer wanted to show that Christ was superior to the angels.

Biblical theologians center their study in three areas: (1) the teachings of a particular book in the Bible or a closely related group of writings, such as the pastoral epistles of the New Testament, or the apocalyptic writings of the Bible (Revelation, Ezekiel, Daniel); (2) the specific historical period of a particular writer and his readers; and (3) distinct factors in the historical situation that may have influenced the writer, the teaching, and the readers.

Biblical theologians are not primarily concerned with trying to make all the teachings of the Bible fit together. Their emphasis is on the nature of a particular teaching and how it feeds the needs of the people at the time it was given.

Biblical and systematic theologians all agree that the Bible itself never gives us a complete essay on the nature of God or on the purpose and nature of the church or on the relationship of God, Son, and Holy Spirit or on any other subject.

Systematic theology emphasizes systems of thought. Systematic theologians try to take all the teachings on a particular subject and put them together to give a full picture of that subject. The emphasis of systematic theologians changes from time to time as pertinent questions change. This is as it should be, for systematic theologians should try to state specific Bible teachings in terms of the problems which people of each generation face. Today's systematic theologians must work with the language and thought patterns of our day. This is not easy. In fact, it is so difficult that systematic theologians often tend to reflect the questions of a bygone era rather than the questions of our own time. Systematic theologies, like Bible translations, must be kept up-to-date if they are to be of greatest use.

To do good work, the systematic theologian must work with the biblical theologian, or at least with that approach. For example, to develop a doctrine of physical creation, we must find out everything the Bible says about God's physical creation: how it came to be, the effect of sin on creation, the future of the physical world. In doing this the systematic theologian must also work with the biblical historical theologian who will be studying, for example, the different meanings of the word *day* in the Bible in various historical settings. He or she must study what the Hebrews meant by the word *formed*, as it is used in the Old Testament describing God's creative activity.

The conscientious systematic theologian cannot formulate a doctrine that cannot be supported by the work of the biblical theologian. He or she must be willing to remain silent when the evidence is not conclusive.

The systematic theologian does similar work on other important subjects—the nature of God, the nature of Christ, etc., taking materials from all parts of the Bible and arranging them in a logical framework that holds together as well as possible the major and minor emphases of the whole Bible.

Systematic theologians must be able to defend

their frameworks of thought. They face these kinds of questions: Why are certain biblical statements given more weight than others? Is it only to give added support to that chosen system? On what grounds does the theologian pick and choose the major teachings of the system? How does he/she put together such teachings as those emphasizing the sovereignty of God and those emphasizing our freedom of choice? How does the teaching of God's sovereignty differ from a rigid determinism in which God causes everything—including the righteous deeds of His people and the sins of His people?

Both biblical and systematic theologies face dangers. Both branches of theology are essential. If we consider theological teachings only in terms of historical backgrounds we may have a history-centered theology with no relevance for today. If we look at teachings only in terms of a logical system of thought we may end up with a human idea-centered theology rather than a biblical one. God can be omitted from either approach.

Even when God is central, neither approach by itself is sufficient. We need the biblical theologian to show how grammatical and historical factors influence doctrinal teachings in particular parts of the Bible in specific periods when God revealed Himself. We need the systematic theologian to bring together all the biblical teachings on a particular subject for our times. For example, how should we present the atonement today to show what is involved in the total meaning?

Ignoring What Does Not Fit the System

Theologians sometimes ignore or play down what does not fit their particular ideas. This is especially tempting to the systematic theologian; but the more he/she knows about the context, grammar, and historical situation of a passage, the better he can analyze and select the relevant teachings and adjust the structure accordingly. He is then less likely to try to make a passage say what the original writer did not intend.

Ignoring context. Some Christians teach by making a statement about their beliefs, followed by a series of verses that supposedly "prove" the statement that has been made. A careful examination of each verse sometimes shows that the passages in their original context and historical situation said little or nothing relating to the statement they are now used to "prove." The method known as "proof-texting" is legitimate and proper only when the interpreter carefully studies each passage in its historical and grammatical context to be sure that it actually teaches the point for which it is now being used. Carelessness in this matter has often brought disrepute to Christianity. The Bible has been "proof-texted" to support racism, sexism, the flat earth, and many other unworthy causes.

Proper proof-texting never quotes a passage to make it say what we want it to say apart from its background.

Unfortunately, many Christians think a book or a speaker is "biblical" if it or the speaker cites many Scripture verses. Many unbiblical teachings have been "proved" by this method. In fact, this practice often gives the reader or listener the impression that the Bible says far more about some subject than it actually says. The reader then thinks he/she knows more about the subject than the Bible actually teaches! This has been particularly true in the area of eschatology—the doctrine of the last days—but it also applies to other subjects.

Attacking those who differ. All Christians, including theologians, are tempted to attack others with whom we disagree. Honest interchange of ideas is usually healthy for the church or for any other group. To condemn other Christians or malign their characters because of some small doctrinal difference is a kind of pride that the Bible strongly condemns. "For while there is jealousy and strife among you, are you not of the flesh, and behaving like ordinary men?" (1 Cor. 3:3).

We all need to admit that the Bible does *not* tell us all we would like to know. It gives us a "sufficient" rule of faith and practice—not a full, "all-knowing" rule.

Because the Bible does not tell us all we would like to know, sincere Christians today say things in different ways and put materials together in different frameworks. Many doctrinal disagreements come from an inherent assumption that each person does or can have the whole picture of truth. The disagreements that arise from our partial knowledge have given doctrine a bad name among many people.

Honesty and humility are needed. An honest biblical scholar tries to consider every passage that actually deals with the subject he is pursuing, but even then some may be missed. Being human, he/she tends to explain some things away and ignore others.

In a limited way each Christian can and should do similar study, and such a Christian will suffer from the same human errors that plague scholars. But we can minimize these problems if we diligently search the Scriptures on any subject in which we are interested, take seriously into account the context and historical situation of the original writer, and then bring together the truths we find to form a "sufficient" rule to live by.

For example, if we make a study of the meaning of sin, we might learn that sin involves a missing of the mark, a revolt against God. It sometimes involves iniquity and pollution, false pride, arrogance, independence. Sin involves attitude and act.

This is not the whole picture of sin in the Bible, but it tells us why we should avoid moral evil. In applying the truths we find, we can be open to a growing understanding of the effects of sin and how we can recognize it. But even if we examine every verse in the Bible that deals with sin, we will still have much left to learn when Christ returns. We do not have the whole picture at the present time.

God has much more to show us. Ephesians 2:7 tells us "that in the ages to come, he might show us the exceeding riches of his grace and his kindness toward us in Christ Jesus" (AT).

The theological topics which most biblical scholars have pursued in past decades may seem a long way from where we live today. Even so, when theology is viewed as truths about God, people, sin, life, and death, then it is indispensable for Christian living.

We must be constantly aware that although we have a divinely inspired Bible, we do NOT have divinely inspired theologies—not Luther's nor Calvin's nor Strong's nor Scofields, nor Barth's nor anyone else's. The source book from which the materials are drawn is divine—the historical or systematic frameworks on which the teachings are hung are clearly human.

Since theological or doctrinal teachings are truths

to live by, they must speak to our particular needs where we are today. We desperately need good theological work on many issues facing the world today such as war and peace, world hunger, the environment, marriage, men-women relationships, work, the material needs of people and our responsibilities to each other.

All theological truth must be growing truth. Because it is so important it warrants our best continuing effort. Every serious Bible student must be involved in *doing* both historical and systematic theology or doctrine.

Questions for Discussion

1. With the help of a concordance, study the references to *saints, sinners,* and the *church* in the book of Revelation.

2. Having looked at all the passages in their literary and historical context, see what doctrines about the church you can formulate from your study.

Chapter 14

Bringing It All Together

"Why should the Bible be so complex?" you may be asking. "Why do I have to distinguish between highest standards and regulations for people where they were? Why didn't God label them for us? Why should I need to study history, culture, language problems, non-Western kinds of poetry, and ancient figures of speech to understand God's message to me?"

You don't necessarily have to. You can read the Bible like any other book, in any version you choose, and much of God's message will come through to you if you read with an open mind, seeking the guidance of the Holy Spirit.

Realistically, however, the Bible is NOT like any other book that has ever been written. It involves many writers, spanning many hundreds of years, writing in languages unknown to us, with thought patterns, customs, and historical situations far removed from us.

Even more important, the Bible is not like any other book because the Bible brings us the *voice of*

God. God is far beyond our most profound thoughts, larger than our most emancipated imaginations, more holy than our sinful minds can comprehend, more loving than we have the capacity to experience.

Even the most devoted student will only scratch the surface of the Bible and its revelations about God and God's dealings with people. The Bible speaks about men and women living and dying, of their tragedies, joys, sins, rebellions against God, reconciliations with God. It speaks of Jesus Christ, God's Son, His life and ministry on this earth, His death, resurrection, His present work on behalf of His people.

Because the Bible is so rich we want to be able to absorb and comprehend as much as possible so that we can grow in our love for God, our obedience to Him, our understanding of ourselves and of the world in which we live.

There are other reasons to be diligent, careful students of the Bible. In our times, sects are multiplying and many are aggressively propagating their beliefs. Most make some use of the Bible in approaching prospective converts. They have a well-designed platter of Bible verses that is served up instantly in response to certain questions.

But most of them have little solid knowledge of the Bible—the kind of knowledge based on the principles outlined in this book.

The Christian who knows only a few scattered Bible verses memorized in childhood is hard-pressed to defend his faith in the face of the many pressures of today.

Actually, the Bible itself does not need to be defended; it only needs to be read and understood and applied by the reader. A genuine solid knowledge of the Bible and how to interpret it frees the Christian from any fears that some new finding will destroy his faith. The truth is not destructible.

Practice is more difficult than theory. It is easier to talk about good principles of interpreting the Bible than it is to practice such principles. This is true of most skills. We can read a text on swimming and learn exactly what our arms and legs are supposed to do in the water. We can even memorize this information. But that does not mean we will be able to swim when we get into the water. Once in the water we discover that mastering the skill is quite different from memorizing the rules.

It takes time and effort to learn to coordinate elements of biblical interpretation involving language, historical backgrounds, culture patterns, figurative language, etc., to arrive at the original meaning of the passage we are studying. It takes additional effort to determine its rightful meaning for us today. We soon find that understanding the Bible, like swimming, is a personal matter. There is no impersonal way to get at its meaning. There are only guidelines to help persons discover meaning.

It often helps to discuss our findings and our methods with fellow Christians from different denominational backgrounds. We may see other views that teach us that our own view is not as absolute as we thought.

If we have already developed bad habits of Bible study, we may feel that it is too difficult to change—too much effort is required. But there is too much at stake to permit us to take the line of least resistance.

The Holy Spirit will help our honest efforts, reprove our faltering willpower, and help us discipline our thinking as we should.

We must account to God for our use of the Bible.

God has given us the Bible as a means through which we may know Him, and we must account to God for our use of it. Jesus said that people will give account on the day of judgment for every idle and useless word (Matt. 12:36). This surely applies to our use of the Bible.

Sincerity will not be an adequate excuse for poor habits when the real problem is laziness or stubbornness.

How we understand the Bible influences not only our lives but also the lives of many around us. If we are aware that we must give account to God for how we interpret His Word, then we must be honest and diligent in our study of it.

God has given us His Word for our growth and for our witness for Him in the world. He has set us free from the domination and penalty of sin. This good news must be brought to every man, woman, and child. To do this, we must understand it.

"The unfolding of thy words gives light; it imparts understanding to the simple [inexperienced]" (Ps. 119:130).

Bibliography: General Helps for the Bible Student

Atlases

Atlas of the Bible, Joseph L. Gardner, ed. Pleasantville, NY: Reader's Digest Association, 1981.

The Macmillan Bible Atlas. Y. Aharoni and M. Avi-Yonah. New York: Macmillan Publishing Co., 1968.

Atlas of the Bible. L.H. Grollenberg. New York: Thomas Nelson, Inc., 1956.

Bible Dictionaries

The Family Bible Encyclopedia, 2 vols. Berkeley and Alvera Mickelsen. Elgin, IL: David C. Cook Publishing Co., 1978.

The New Bible Dictionary. J.D. Douglas, et al. Grand Rapids: Wm. B. Eerdmans Publishing Co., 1962.

Pictorial Bible Dictionary. Merrill Tenney. Grand Rapids: Zondervan Publishing House, 1967.

Bible Commentaries

The Daily Study Bible Series. William Barclay. Philadelphia: Westminster Press. (This is a series of books on the New Testament that is particularly helpful on matters of history and culture of the New Testament period.)

Great People of the Bible and How They Lived. Pleasantville, NY: Reader's Digest Association, 1974.

The New Bible Commentary, rev. Guthrie, Moyer, Stibbs, Wiseman. Grand Rapids: Wm. B. Eerdmans Publishing Co., 1970.

The Wycliffe Bible Commentary. Pfeiffer and Harrison. Chicago: Moody Press, 1962.